Dancers!
Assume the Position

THE WHAT, THE WHY, AND THE IMPACT OF THE DANCER'S MINISTRY

2nd Edition

Marlita S. Hill

ISBN 978-0-615-81762-0

First Printing: 2008

Dancing Hill Ministries

http://thedancersministry.com

facebook.com/dancersministry

Printed in the United States of America

Acknowledgements

To my Mom (Pamela Watson) and Dad (Ronald Hill), thank you for being amazing parents. To my bro-ham (Ronald), lil' scrappy (Neshea), and my mini-me (Jannelle), I love you guys very much!

Pastor Paul and Victoria, thank you for your years of friendship, investment, and encouragement. Pastor Troy, I appreciate you taking the time to read and proof this book. I honor your integrity, sir.

Julie McManus, thank you first of all for being so patient and gracious with me during this process. Thank you for the amazingly beautiful artwork! I get so excited every time I look at it. You have helped make this book all that God showed me it would be. Thank you, thank you, thank you!

To my Besties: Nycole, Elaine, Cristina, Fifi, Tamie, Michelle, Elisa, Charlotte, and Elizabeth, I love you ladies more than I could possibly say. Thank you for being such amazing women!

Fallynne and Sylvia, I love you guys to life! Thank you for letting me cut my teeth as a leader. Thank you for letting me be vulnerable and admit when I didn't know what to do. Thank you for keeping your commitment and pushing through with me.

Annabel, Mya, and Jeanne, what could I possibly say to you three that could begin to express how critical and healing you have been to my life and my assignment in this season. I am so grateful that God brought us together. Thank you for your hearts, your love for God, your belief in me and in the assignment God has given me. I pray God's blessing and favor overtake your life as a harvest on all the seed you have sown into my mine.

Pastor Hoss, you are such a man of God, and such a man of integrity. I thank you for your friendship and for welcoming me into your family. Thank you for always making yourself available to speak to me when I need it. I honor you, sir, and I pray God's blessing and favor continually increase on your life and your family.

*Stacy and LaQuin Meadows and
Bishop Clarence E. McClendon:
You will never fully understand what your leadership and instruction has done in me- how it has forever changed the course and quality of my life. Thank you for undertaking the necessary life sacrifices that enabled you to hear from God and so diligently pour into my hungry spirit. I am forever grateful.*

Testimonials

If you have ever been, are currently in, or even thinking about being in dance ministry, I HIGHLY RECOMMEND this book for your dancer's library. Marlita's writing is easy to read and understand, and it is filled with scripture, personal stories, and sound principles for anyone in worship dance ministry. If you dance for the Lord and want to take your dance to the next level for God's great glory, then "Assume the Position" is a necessity. Moreover, as a worship arts pastor, I was also challenged and encouraged by this book. You don't have to be a dancer to derive sound, Biblical principles for your ministry from this book! Read and be blessed! *Jody T Schultz*

This is a book for people who have reached the absolute end- who ask is this all there is to Christianity- and want more. *Carol Walker*

I recommend this book to anyone who is desiring a closer relationship with God through the vehicle of dance. To the praise dancer starting out in his or her journey or to the seasoned dancer, this book is for you. I liked how it talked about how important prayer and seeking God in every aspect of your journey… we dance because of JESUS !!! It is an easy book to read and you can tell it is God inspired. *Jeanne Karas*

I have this book and I use it as a resource. Every dancer should have a copy of this book. Personally and prophetically inspiring. Marlita shares her great insight of the dance ministry and how we communicate the very Word of God through our dance. Our bodies used to influence others and be inspired can be a powerful vehicle to communicate a gracious message. *April*

As soon as I started to read this book I didn't want to put it down. It answered so many questions I was thinking. I had been praying for more direction and God lead me to this book! What is Dance Ministry? Why Dance? How God uses us in Dance Ministry for His purpose and so much more! I have a better understanding as to what the Lord needs from me as a Dancer for His purpose. Many scriptures were given to reference and reflect upon. Easy read. It's a book you want to read over and over again. Thank you Marlita for allowing God to use you to write this book. It has ministered to me and I know it will minster to many. *Annabel Taylor*

I have this book & have read it many times. I refer to it constantly. It has answered every question I ever had regarding dance, & how to let God lead in the choreography and the garment. I highly recommend this book to anyone. It is easy reading and not confusing. This is an excellent resource for the beginner in the Worship Art of Dance. *Sue*

This book is more than thought-provoking. It has unbound my creativity and moved me to another level, while reinforcing what I knew about my purpose in dance. I will now use this book as required reading in my dance ministry workshops and teachings. *Loretta Green*

This book has been needed for many years in the dance ministry community. I encourage everyone who has a heart to worship God to read it. It will take you to another level. *Nycole Jones*

A must read! Anointed and revelatory. I would recommend "Dancers! Assume the Position" even to those who do not dance. This book is a good book to read even if you serve in a different capacity. *LaQuin Meadows*

"Dancers! Assume the Position" is a "must have" for anyone involved in, or considering dance ministry. It is clear, concise and well researched. After 13 years of dance ministry, I have never found another resource like it!
Victoria Castanos, Revolution Dance and Performing Arts

Dancers! Assume the Position has totally changed my view of dance, my ministry, and quite frankly my life. This book is a must read for all ministers, not just dancing ministers! Marlita has a way of breaking down the Bible and complex subjects so that it is easy to understand. I love her use of analogies and down to earth talk. She completely connects and gets straight to the heart of the matter about ministry and WHY we dance. One of my favorite quotes is " The true quest is to stay presented, which is a journey, made of opportunity-by-opportunity decisions to obey God when he speaks." Yes! Simply said this book is a must have, especially for ministry leaders! I promise if you read it, receive it, and implement it, your understanding, passion, and ministry will go to the another level!" *Theresita Rouse Richard*

A splendid arrangement of revelation knowledge! *Stacy Meadows*

THANK YOU LORD!!! I must say – when God answers a prayer, He truly comes through. I am so excited about this book I could scream. The spirit-filled writing, organization of ideas, obvious consideration in choice of words are just some of the reasons this book has made it to my "best of the best" collection! *Mya Hines*

Contents

Preface

Right information is of great use as to all religious practice. It is wretched work, which gifted men make, who either do not know, or do not advert to the nature and right use of the gifts with which they are endowed.
Matthew Henry Commentary.

When I read that quote, I think of the gift we have been endowed with: the privilege of being able to use the dance to participate in God's purpose.

I first experienced dance ministry in 1994, while working at the BOSS[1] carnival in the Idyllwild Mountains of California. An announcement came over the loud speaker that a dance group would be performing in a few minutes. Disinterested, I ignored the announcement. Suddenly this voice spoke in my ear, "Go watch." I ignored the voice. I had seen dance groups before and I wasn't interested in seeing this one. Again the voice spoke, "Go watch," and this time it was accompanied by a tiny, nudging feeling. I stood there. A third time the voice commanded me to go and watch the group. Finally relenting, I very resentfully asked my friend to go with me to watch the dancers. I plopped into the chair, arms haughtily crossed, waiting to see the grand display.

The group was introduced and they entered the stage. They were called The Hush Company- a Los Angeles based dance ministry under the direction of Stacy and LaQuin Meadows. Prior to that moment, I had never heard of dance ministry. My friends and I used to make up cheers and dances and perform them in the church, but I had no idea that dance could actually be used to minister to people and affect their lives. It is still hilarious to remember myself sitting in that chair, too foolish to perceive that I was staring destiny in the face. I had no clue that God was about to rock my world.

The music started to play. They ministered a piece entitled "I Am Here," by Commissioned. The first to dance was LaQuin, who did a dramatic portrayal of a girl who had lost hope, falling into alcoholism and about to attempt to kill herself. As she held the gun to her head, Stacy, representing

---

[1] Building On Spiritual Substance: A word-based training that teaches youth to be entrepreneurs. Headed by Al and Hattie Hollingsworth of Christian Business Ministries.

Jesus, came forward and began to minister to her through the words of the song. I sat there, glued to my chair. I don't think I ever blinked. As I continued to watch, my chest tightened and tears began to stream down my face. My hands began to tremble and I felt this tremendous weight on my chest. I was so overtaken by what I was seeing. Everyone else around me disappeared and it was as if it was just me, the dancers, and God on top of that big mountain. After their performance I got a chance to meet The Hush Company and a week later I became a member.

Over the next eight years God would use Stacy and LaQuin to teach me about purpose, calling, and the ministry of dance. They diligently and freely poured into me and, like a hungry baby, I greedily consumed everything they put before me. I learned what happened in the process of ministry through dance, what was affecting these people and what was being done inside of them. Traveling and ministering with them enabled me to see that my mountain experience was not an isolated incident. People all over the country were being touched by the presence of God through this dance ministry experience. I had seen dance before, but never had I seen or experienced an effect like that of The Hush Company. There arose in me a curiosity about what I was witnessing. Something was inherently different in this organism called dance ministry and I wanted to know what it was. And yet, the more information I received, the more questions I had. What I was insanely curious to understand were the how's and why's. Why does God use the dance? What is it about the dance that He finds so useful in reaching His people? How does ministry happen through the dance? I knew *that* it happened, but how? What I wanted was for God to lift up the hood and walk me through how this machine ran: the parts of the machine, what they were connected to and what made each part function. So I set my life to understand it.

The first place I started was, of course, the Bible. At first glance, it does not give much information about dance. There are no direct or obvious standpoints or instructions regarding it, besides Psalms 149 and 150. The few references and occurrences of dance in scripture offer little to no immediate insight beyond the fact that it was very much a part of the existence of the people. No explanation is given as to why it is important to dance, what the affects are, how it works, or where the dancer fits in the purposes of God. Still, despite the lack of references where the dancer is directly addressed, experience has demonstrated that the dance is in fact a vehicle that God is more than willing to use for His glory and endorse with His power.

Several years ago, God began to teach me about dance ministry based on principles outlined in the word. He dealt with me about looking at it in a context greater than the 5-10 minutes we spend ministering before the people of God. This season of instruction became the catalyst for this book. He gave me the phrase "Dancers! Assume the Position!" as He taught me that there is a position we must assume that is more fundamental than that of a dancer. In fact, this most fundamental position informs what we do as dancers in ministry. This book seeks to discover and understand that position, and the context of dance within it.

As you read this book you will find no discussion about how you should dance, what you should or should not dance to, what colors you should wear, what part of your body you shouldn't move, etc. I am more interested in what makes our dance usable to God in His purpose, and what qualifies what we do in the dance as ministry. I sincerely believe that if we focus on fulfilling ministry as it is laid forth in this book, we will be fully within the will of God, no matter what we wear or how we move.

I do not presume to know how your ministry should be run or structured, nor do I have any other specifics concerning your individual assignment. God, however, does have the specific details of your assignment through dance; and He is more than ready to share them with you. This book is only designed to provide general context for our place and function within His purposes, and to show why it is so important to make regular consultation with Him a can't-function-without-it part of the life of your ministry. Besides the guidelines in this book, I believe that He purposely gave little direction for how to structure our individual dance ministries because the pursuit and accomplishment of individual ministry cannot come through a generic guidebook. Real and true God-directed ministry is only produced through individual relationship and collaboration with the Holy Spirit.

I pray that you find liberty in these pages. I pray that you gain a deeper understanding of what God intended for the dance, and what He, in using the dance, intended to uniquely produce through you when He specifically chose you as a way to show Himself to the world.

"Dancers! Assume the Position" is so biblical, so well-organized, and so well-articulated, that everyone in leadership or aspiring to enter ministry should have this book in hand. I would suggest that you read it three times. Read it rapidly to grasp the wealth of information. Then, read it thoughtfully to understand its principles. And finally, read it intentionally to put the information and principles into practice.

Pastor Phillip Hoss
New Life Church, Temecula, CA

v

How to Use this Book

Well, first let me start by qualifying the nature of this book. It is not a training manual. It is a study guide. It is information that establishes a context and challenges you to ponder, discover, and frame your place within that context. This book is a lens that, from now on, will target and focus how you see and define yourself as a dance minister, how you study about ministry through dance, how you pray about it, train your dancers, discuss it, and how you communicate the nature and value of what you do to others.

Take this information and meditate on it. Talk about it. Commune with God over it. Take the scriptures and reflection questions into your prayer time and bible study. Incorporate them into the training for your ministry. Read this book. And read it again. And read it again and again. Set aside time once a year to re-read it as a ministry in order to refresh and realign yourselves in relationship with God, and in the assignment He gave you. The fact is that there is so much more that God wants to show you about your dance in Him – more than I could ever possibly set my mind to comprehend or my hands to write. Use this book to help you assume, and maintain, your position.

1
Ministry Demystified

Mighty dancers of the Lord, what was God's intention when He committed this powerful vehicle into our care? Within that intention, what makes our dance usable in His purpose? As we set forth to answer this, let us first agree on a working definition for dance in this capacity. We have coined many names for it: praise dance, worship dance, Christian dance, liturgical dance, etc. I believe these various names come out of our attempt to best articulate and define what it is that we do when we stand before the people of God. For the purpose of our discussion, I will refer to what we do as dance ministry, or ministry through dance.

> *The dance is not the ministry and the ministry is not the dance.*

What is dance ministry? The Spirit of God gave me the following definition: **Dance ministry is the process of using dance as a vehicle to carry out the act of ministry**. This definition brings to light a very important distinction: the dance is not the ministry and the ministry is not the dance. In fact, they are two separate and distinct entities. Dance ministry is actually a relationship created by the coming together of ministry and the gift of

1

dance. This same relationship between ministry and gift exists for every post of ministry. Preaching, for example, is the relationship created by the coming together of ministry and the gift of speaking. The function of worship leader is the coming together of ministry and the gift of singing.

Separating the two begs for clarification, as dancing does not necessarily mean we are also ministering. Though God has called us to it, the dance is only the vehicle we have been given to use in fulfilling our ministry. If dance is the vehicle, what is the ministry? When we talk about ministry we like to present it as this deep and ethereal experience, as if revealing its simplicity diminishes its relevance or potency. It is not what many of us have thought it to be, and much simpler than we have supposed.

A preliminary word study reveals that ministry is basically the rendering of service. Its various Hebrew and Greek definitions differ in the type of service rendered, where it is provided, who renders the service, and who directs the service. But, at its bare essence ministry is plain and simply service. Webster's Unabridged Dictionary defines service as "an act done for the benefit or at the command of another." A servant is "a person in the employ and subject to the direction of an individual or company; some[one] that serves the purposes of another." To serve is to "be of help in bringing about, or to be of use or answer the needs of." These definitions reveal two characteristics of service:

The principle of finding out and bringing what is being asked for is central to the discussion of ministry.

1. It serves to benefit and assist in someone else's purpose.
2. It is generally performed at the command or direction of that person.

There is a difference between service and effort. Effort is "the expenditure of energy to accomplish some objective."[2] Where effort expends energy to accomplish *some* objective, service expends energy to fulfill a directed task. To demonstrate the difference, let's say I ask you to hand me a hammer. You hand me a screwdriver. Have you served me, or have you made an effort towards me? Both handing me the hammer and the screwdriver are

---

[2] www.dictionary.com

expenditures of energy, but service requires that your energy be applied to producing what I have directed or requested. What, then, would serve me? For you to hand me the hammer, to hand me what I asked for. This principle of **"what I asked for"** is central to the discussion of ministry and can be further illustrated by looking at the nature of the service business.

The Business of Service

The essence of operating a business in the service industry is to *proceed as directed*. These businesses are built around the wants and needs of customers, which are made known through the services they request. They are different from retail businesses where consumer goods such as books, food, clothes, and music are sold. Retail businesses, like Vons Supermarket, Target, and Barnes & Nobles are stocked with consumer goods and they operate on customers selecting the goods they want and purchasing them. Service businesses, like Kinko's, mechanics, and hair salons have no consumer goods to sell. They sell their services (styling hair, fixing cars, or making copies). These businesses do not produce any "products" until a customer comes in and purchases the application of their service.

In retail, customers come for products that are already assembled, packaged, and ready for purchase. If I go into Barnes & Nobles all that is required of me is to make a decision as to whether or not I want to purchase the books or CD's they have in stock.

Conversely, service businesses offer the raw materials I need to produce what I want, and from them I purchase specificity: the application of their skills and materials to generate a product or result that has been tailored to my request. For instance, I want 50 custom-made invitations for my party. A retail business, like Target, will have 50 invitations in their store, but they won't be custom-made because generalization is the nature of retail business. Instead, I will have to choose from the selection of pre-made invitations available in their store. To get the specific invitations I want, I would instead go to a service business, like Kinko's. However, Kinko's will not have 50 custom-made invitations sitting on a shelf *there*, either. To get my custom invitations, I have to tell a Kinko's employee specifically what I want on them, how I want them designed and laid out, and that I want 50 of them made on green paper. Upon receiving my instructions, Kinko's will then employ their skills and materials to producing not just anything, but specifically what I ordered. If I come back to Kinko's to pick up my order and they give me 40 invitations on red paper, they have not done their job because their business is to employ their resources in compliance with the specifications I, the customer, requested.

In this regard, God is our customer and our business is to employ our resources (gifts, talents, and abilities) towards providing service in compliance with His specifications.

This implies two things:

- Before we do anything, we must first consult with our Customer to see what He wants us to produce for Him.
- We should not be producing anything until we have specifications to employ our resources towards.

It would be bad business and a waste of resources for Kinko's to make random batches of specialized invitations for the sake of appearing busy. As a service business, it is more cost-effective for them to refrain from printing any material until they actually receive an order.

This idea of stillness is counter to Western culture. There is a time to move and a time to be still. And yet, being still is not always valued in American society where activity is synonymous with progress and productivity, no matter how unfruitful the activity may be; and where stillness is perceived as laziness and unproductiveness. We must overcome the anxiety of being still and resist the pressure we feel to *do something*. This can be difficult in our present church culture, which measures success on how big our ministry is and how often we are booked, regardless of the timeliness and fruitfulness of our labors. We feel compelled to say "yes" every time we are asked, perhaps for fear that people will stop asking or because we feel an obligation to always go when requested. We continue to say "yes" even when we feel that still small voice telling us to say "no" for a season; even when we know we haven't been given anything to say; even when we have reached the point of exhaustion and "let's just do..." or "they haven't seen this one in a while so let's do..." becomes the way that we choose what we deliver to the people of God. We continue to say "yes," all the while forgetting with every "yes," that our service is not to be booked. Our service is to produce what our Customer has requested.

What, then, has our Customer asked for? What has He whispered into our hearts and compelled us to use our resources to bring to Him? It is something much more fundamental than the dance, and actually informs how we utilize the dance.

Dance Ministry In Grace

In the first edition of this book, I proceeded to make the case that obedience is what God is seeking from us, providing scripture to substantiate this truth. Recently, however, Bishop Clarence E. McClendon[3] has been teaching about understanding and living in our covenant, about understanding how God relates to us and how we are to relate to Him based on the covenant we live under – "a better covenant built on better promises (Heb. 8:6)." The revelation and understanding from that teaching demanded that I come back and restructure how I presented this section. Two things from the teaching stood out to me that pertain to our conversation:

1) God never wanted man to just obey Him. He wanted man to believe Him. McClendon further clarified this truth, explaining that "you can obey someone and not believe them; but if you believe them, you will obey them."

God does need our obedience, but the obedience He is after is one borne out of believing Him and coming into agreement with Him through our actions. He is not after obedience as we have traditionally understood it: an obedience borne out of obligation, to try to earn His goodness, to try to get something from Him, or for fear that He will punish us or take something from us if we don't obey Him.

2) Referencing 1 Cor. 10:11, he taught that everything in the Old Covenant is to be understood by us, but not necessarily to be performed by us. The Old Covenant is for our instruction and our example and it reveals principles that teach us something about our God.

In this understanding, let's see what insight the scriptures give us about obeying God.

---

[3] Bishop Clarence E. McClendon is the Senior Pastor of Full Harvest International in Gardena,CA. http://bishopmcclendon.com

Jer. 7:22-23 (AMP)

"For in the day that I brought them out of the land of Egypt, I did not speak to your fathers or command them concerning burnt offerings or sacrifices. But this thing I did command them: Listen to *and* obey My voice, and I will be Your God and you will be My people; and walk in the whole way that I command you, that it may be well with you."

1 Sam. 15:22 (KJV)

"And Samuel said, 'Hath the LORD as great delight in burnt offerings and sacrifices, as in obeying the voice of the LORD? Behold, to obey is better than sacrifice, and to hearken than the fat of rams.'"

Hosea 6:6 (AMP)

"For I desire *and* delight in dutiful steadfast love *and* goodness, not sacrifice, and the knowledge of *and* acquaintance with God more than burnt offerings."

Eccl. 5:1 (AMP)

"Keep your foot [give your mind to what you are doing] when you go [as Jacob to sacred Bethel] to the house of God. For to draw near to hear *and* obey is better than to give the sacrifice of fools [carelessly, irreverently] too ignorant to know that they are doing evil."

Mk. 12:28-33 (KJV)

"And one of the scribes came, and having heard them reasoning together, and perceiving that he had answered them well, asked him, Which is the first commandment of all? And Jesus answered him, The first of all the commandments is, Hear, O Israel; The Lord our God is one Lord: And thou shalt love the Lord thy God with all thy heart, and with all thy soul, and with all thy mind, and with all thy strength: this is the first commandment. And the second is like, namely this, Thou shalt love thy neighbour as thyself. There is none other commandment greater than these. And the scribe said unto him, Well, Master, thou hast said the truth: for there is one God; and there is none other but he: And to love him with all the heart, and with all the understanding, and with all the soul, and with all the strength, and to love his neighbour as himself, is more than all whole burnt offerings and sacrifices."

Now before you get excited, let's see how God determines if we love Him.

John 14:23, 24 (NKJV)

"Jesus answered and said to him, 'If anyone loves Me, he will keep My word; and My Father will love him, and We will come to him and make Our home with him. He who does not love Me does not keep My words; and the word which you hear is not Mine but the Father's who sent Me.'"

I found it striking in the first four verses how much God desires to commune with us, not to just bark orders at us. He desires for us to know who He is, what He wants, what He's involved in, and what pleases Him. Many times, because God is not visible to our natural eye, we forget that He is still a person. Yes, He is Supreme Master, Creator, and Lord of the universe but He is still a person, and we are in relationship with Him, the person.

Have you ever received a gift from someone and you knew that they put no thought into it, as if they could have just randomly picked it up off the street and given it to you? It is difficult to feel appreciative of the gift when that happens. God feels the same way. It is as if He is saying, *I want your knowledge of Me and understanding of My will to be the catalyst to all that you do for Me. I want you to seek first what I have asked for, what I desire, what pleases Me and allow that to guide you.*

Isa. 1:11-17 (NKJV)

"To what purpose is the multitude of your sacrifices to Me?" Says the Lord. "I have had enough of burnt offerings of rams and the fat of fed cattle. I do not delight in the blood of bulls, Or of lambs or goats. "When you come to appear before Me, Who has required this from your hand, to trample My courts? Bring no more futile sacrifices; Incense is an abomination to Me. The New Moons, the Sabbaths, and the calling of assemblies—I cannot endure iniquity and the sacred meeting. Your New Moons and your appointed feasts My soul hates; They are a trouble to Me, I am weary of bearing them. When you spread out your hands, I will hide My eyes from you; Even though you make many prayers, I will not hear. Your hands are full of blood. "Wash yourselves, make yourselves clean; Put away the evil of your doings from before My eyes. Cease to do evil, Learn to do good; seek justice, rebuke the oppressor; defend the fatherless, plead for the widow."

This is an interesting passage because the very institutions that God condemns here are institutions that He, Himself, set up. The only reason the children of Israel were doing those things in the first place was in obedience to His command. So, what happened? What changed? Why were these activities suddenly so offensive to Him?

As soon as we begin to pay more attention to procedure and result than we pay to the proceeding Word, we have fallen into ritual.

During the Spirit of Prophecy Conference 2012, McClendon taught the foundations (Strongs: the reasons why) in our walk with God must be "rediscovered and properly applied in each generation by revelation [because] the revelation on [those] foundations shift to be relevant to the current culture."

Though God commanded them to be done, the ordinances in themselves had no merit. The **obedience** to the ordinances **at God's word** was, and remains, the whole point of the matter. In this passage, God is addressing a people who are continuing in the same activities, but have reduced what was birthed out of communion and agreement down to ceremony (doing it "this way" because we've always done it "this way") and product (anything birthed out of time with God, i.e. method, strategy, instruction, a dance, etc). They believed that simply replicating the activity that was handed down to them would bring them the same results. This was dangerous business because products have an expiration date and they were never designed to render the Creator unnecessary. These people in Isa. 1:11-17 had made three major errors:

1. They did not seek God about the place, application, and even necessity of these ceremonies in their generation.
2. They created sanctity around the ceremonies and elevated that above the true sanctity of the connection to their Source.

3. They allowed ceremony and product to stop their pursuit of God and His proceeding Word.

They had fallen into ritual. Ritual is problematic because it is about trying to establish yourself as fit or worthy because of your activity, rather than because you have aligned your activity with God's word. It attributes the source of the power to the doer or the activity done, instead of to the real Source.

How does this apply to us as dancers? Where are we prone to exalt ceremony and product in the doing of ministry? Some areas that came to mind are:

- Raising garments, colors, and instruments too far above their part in the bigger picture,

- Being led more by our technical training and dance knowledge than the direction of the Holy Spirit,

- Staunch adherence to the way we've always done things in our ministries (like select songs, run rehearsals, choreograph dances, etc). In December 2012, Dr. Mark Hanby came and spoke to our leadership about the critical necessity of pliability in ministry. Among the many powerful things he shared, one statement really brought me to attention. He said, "we kill our promise and live in death doing exactly what God said to do because we did not hear the proceeding Word." Though we initially seek God about these matters, it is important for us to stay sensitive to His leading as we move through seasons and dimensions of purpose.

- Lastly, the way we view the role of dance in what we do.

There are two ways to view dance in ministry. One viewpoint holds that the dance *is* the ministry. If dance *is* the ministry, then simply dancing makes you obedient. This thinking looks at dance ritualistically, removing us from the responsibility of having to pursue the proceeding Word (to find out what is being asked for and bring that). It does not require us to consult God or comply with Him in any part of the process. It just requires us to do the activity of dance and merits us based on how much we dance.

The other viewpoint holds dance simply as what is used to *fulfill* ministry, requiring us to continually go and find out what is being asked of us and to comply. Matthew 4:4 (KJV) tells us that "man shall not live by bread alone, but by every word that proceedeth out of the mouth of God." As soon as we begin to pay more attention to procedure and result than we pay to the proceeding Word, we have fallen into ritual.

The small sampling of scripture that preceded shows that God is very clear about what He wants from us. The one thing that matters most to Him, that pleases Him more, that serves Him best is when we believe Him and come into agreement with Him. Yes, it is that simple- He just wants belief and agreement, out of which flows obedience.

How meticulously we obey God in the activity of dance, then, is much more important than the supposed "holiness" of our movements or garments. A posture of obedience would actually require that we seek God *concerning* our garments and movements.

Religion has devised a process and notion of ministry that is comprised of many activities that have the appearance of being "for God," but consist only of what we think He'd want, without regard for the one thing He asked for; or, as Dr. Hanby pointed out, we continue in what He want**ed**, completely oblivious to His present leading. This mentality creeps into our doings for God when we forget, after He has manifested Himself, that His response was to our act of obedience, not to the activity itself. Why is our obedience so important to God?

"Starting from the Finish"[4] has taught me the importance of
1. Having the correct understanding of my partnership with God, and
2. Understanding where, how, and why obedience fits into that relationship.

As we quoted earlier, McClendon taught that God was after belief more than He was after obedience; understanding that obedience is a natural by-product of belief. The New International Dictionary of New Testament Theology, Vol 1., explains that "belief (gr. *pisteuo*)" refers to "a personal relationship with a person or thing which is established by trust or trustworthiness." From God's stand point, our obedience is a matter of

---

[4] A message taught by Bishop Mc Clendon in July 2013

creating agreement within a personal relationship established by and in trust, not about exacting subservience. If He just wanted subservience from us, He would have created us like the angels, who have no choice *but* to obey Him when He speaks. Yet He didn't.

Instead, He took the first step toward us to show Himself worthy of our trust. His faith is that as we get to know Him – His character, His ability, His love and plan for us – that we would come to trust Him, growing in reverence, love, and admiration for Him. His faith is that this cycle of trust and trustworthiness would produce in us a heart towards Him that says: *I love You so much and I trust You so much that I'm here because You're here; and I want to be wherever You are. I'm here to do whatever You want me to do because I want to be a part of whatever You're doing.* This is agreement-obedience, the manner of obedience that God desires.

If we are to be effective in ministry, we must settle the following within ourselves:

1. God brings us into a finished work.

By the time we get involved, what the work is and is to look like has already been determined. It already has an identity, specific aim and purpose, leaving us to simply proceed as directed to manifest it in the earth.

2. We are in God's purpose.

As we learned earlier, the nature of service is that it is employed to help bring about *someone else's* purpose. The thing about help is that only the person receiving the help can determine whether the things being done for them are truly helping them. If I intend to be of help, I first need to communicate with the one I will be helping to find out what they need and how they desire to be helped. This changes the way I approach helping. Now, I do not assume that anything that I do will necessarily be of help. Instead, I listen for what they really need. I also do not hold the expectation that they should be grateful for whatever I throw their way because I understand that I am not there to simply be active in their presence, but to help them in the way that *they* need.

3. God needs our agreement to get His purpose accomplished in the earth.

In Genesis 1, God set man to have dominion over all the earth. This means that He, who wants to establish His kingdom in the earth, cannot do so without our participation because He gave to us the authority to determine what can and cannot happen here. Breathe. He set it up that way. Agreement-obedience is, therefore, necessary because it requires us to agree on an outcome and fulfill directives that will produce what was agreed on. When God calls us to participate with Him in ministry, then, He calls us with the intention of us coming into agreement with what He is doing and setting ourselves to producing *that* thing. Even as dancers, we are drafted to use the dance to further what He is after. We are working to further His agenda, thus agreeing to follow His directives. He, alone, knows what will be needed and seeks His sons to help Him bring it forth. God seeks presented vessels.

A Presented Disposition

Rom. 12:1 (AMP):

"I appeal to you therefore, brethren, and beg of you in view of [all] the mercies of God, to make a decisive dedication of your bodies [presenting all your members and faculties] as a living sacrifice, holy (devoted, consecrated) and well-pleasing to God, which is your reasonable (rational, intelligent) service and spiritual worship."

For me, this verse brings attention to the posture I must assume to truly serve God in ministry. As I thought about the idea of being a "living sacrifice," I struggled to understand what Paul meant until I examined his request in parts. I first discovered that the word "living" is a verb, not an adjective, and does not describe what type of sacrifice, as in living or dead, but instead describes what the sacrifice is *to do*. With "living" as a verb the verse could be rewritten as: Present your bodies as a sacrifice **to live, or that will live** holy and acceptable to God, which is your reasonable service. Many of us, including myself, have only partially presented ourselves because we have been ambiguous in our understanding of what it really means to be presented.

The church has long been victim to theological grandiloquence[5] and sesquipedalianism[6] (I meant that to sound ridiculous) and has lost sight of the powerful practicality needed to successfully walk out what we know. We have regarded the act of presenting as merely a verbal action that is, in itself, a destination. But, it is not. After our emotional dedication to God and our fervent request to be used, after we dry our tears and peel ourselves off of the floor there is still that next and necessary step.

The word *present* partially comes from another word that means "to cause a person or a thing to keep his or its place."[7] The true quest is to *stay* presented, which is a journey, made of opportunity-by-opportunity decisions to obey God when He speaks. I looked up the definition for "present" and I was intrigued by how much it complemented the disposition of service and obedience. To present is:

- To place a person or thing at one's disposal (*which means the receiver - the one being presented to - has the power and liberty to arrange, place, or set that which was presented to them however they wish*).
- To be at hand, or
- To stand by to help (*which means being ready and available to act- for someone else's cause*).[8]

What do these definitions imply? If I place something at your disposal, including myself, I am giving you the authority to decide and execute what you want with what I presented to you, without my interference, and despite my objection. I cannot truly present something to you and then dictate its use. If I put restrictions on it, I have not really presented it to you. I have simply let you hold it, and have given you the false impression that I have entrusted it to you.

Presenting ourselves is much like being hired as a Target employee. When I accept their job offer, I am placing how my hours will be spent there at the disposal of Target management. When I clock into work on Monday morning, I must check in with management to see how they have designated for me to spend my time that day. I must then set myself to

---

[5] excessive use of verbal ornamentation (www.dictionary.com)
[6] The overuse of long words (www.dictionary.com)
[7] Histemi, Strong's #2476
[8] www.crosswalk.com

whatever they've determined as one who, in accepting the job, has voluntarily presented myself, my time, and my talents to them. If I want to stay employed by Target, I must carry that same disposition every time I clock in to work. As long as I work for them, I must bring my work activity into agreement with their decisions because I am employed in *their* business.

Jesus beautifully exemplified this notion in the way He understood and conducted His earthly ministry. Through Isaiah 61, we know that Jesus' ministry was to preach good tidings to the poor, to heal the brokenhearted, to proclaim liberty to the captives and the opening of the prison to those who are bound. What we overlook, however, and fail to replicate in our own ministry is that though Jesus knew the activities He was to do, and the vehicles He was to do them through, those activities and vehicles were submitted to a higher principle. If you study Jesus' ministry, you will find that He did not just bust through Israel healing whoever He wanted, preaching whatever He wanted, wherever He wanted. Christ, the very Word made flesh, the Son of God who was prophesied about from the beginning of time, operated under restrictions. He discloses the principles that restricted all His ministerial activity.

John 5:19 (NKJV)
"Most assuredly, I say to you, the Son can do nothing of Himself, but what He sees the Father do; for whatever He does, the Son does also in like manner."

John 12:49 (NKJV)
"For I have not spoken on My own authority; but the Father who sent Me gave Me a command, what I should say and what I should speak."

John 14:10 (NKJV)
"The words that I speak to you I do not speak on My own authority; but the Father who dwells in Me does the works."

In John 5:30 and 8:28, Christ, the Son of God, our wonderful Savior, admits at least twice that He cannot do anything by Himself, and that he only proceeds through the instruction of the Father because it is the Father's will that He came to fulfill. He understood that His first ministry was to attend to and align Himself with the words of His Father, and that the actions of stretching out His hand to heal, or opening His mouth to preach and teach were simply *means* to fulfill what He heard. In the same way, our actual ministry is to attend to and align ourselves with the voice of our Father. Dance is the vehicle we use to carry out what we receive while attending to Him in ministry.

Remember the encounter between Jesus and the Canaanite woman who wanted Him to deliver her daughter?[9] He told her that He could not do what she asked. This is interesting because she asked Him to do something that He Himself declared was a part of his assignment. Why, then, did He initially say "no" to her? Because, Jesus understood that obeying God about *what* to do with the activity of healing took precedence over the activity of healing itself. He understood that His stewardship of healing people had to stay within the parameters set by His Father because He was only doing these things to fulfill His Father's will. He initially said "no" to the woman because He was only sent to the children of Israel and she was not a child of Israel, even though what she asked was in the realm of His assignment. The point is *she* was not in the realm of His assignment and He had to submit to a principle greater than the action of putting His hand on someone's head.

We have looked at several important issues as it relates to the general conduct and disposition needed in ministry. How does this all apply to the dancer?

In all that we have established thus far, there are three key points to revisit as we apply ministry to the dance:

> *There is something bigger than the dance, beyond the dance, and yet including the dance, that we have been enlisted to exercise care over.*

---

[9] Mt. 15:21-28

1. The dance is not our ministry. Our ministry is to attend to the Father, and align ourselves with that which He leads us to do with and through the dance.
2. The dance is a vehicle that has He has entrusted to us for the purpose of fulfilling our assignment *in His will.*
3. Like the job offer, we voluntarily accept our assignment and choose to walk in agreement-obedience because we respect and acknowledge that we are handling His business.

These ideas of entrusting and intended use make me think of a company vehicle. If you are an employee of my company and I let you use the company car, I am giving you temporary custody and stewardship of the car so that you can use it to take care of the things I need you to take care of for my business. I am not putting the car in your care for you to go get your hair done, to go grocery shopping, or take a road trip. I may give you permission to use the car for those purposes, but only if they do not interfere with you first making sure you handle company business. In ministry, we sometimes fall into the trap of confusing stewardship with ownership. This is understandable because we take on a sense of ownership with the gift and assignment we have been given. We make them our own and we take personal responsibility for them; but this feeling of ownership must be held in proper context. How, then, do we handle that which is not ours? How do we regard the person to whom what we hold belongs? Through agreement-obedience.

Ownership does not require you to give account to anyone because you are dealing with your own stuff. Stewardship, however, does require accountability and an acknowledgement that the things you deal with are, in fact, not your own, even though the one who entrusted it to you wishes you to guard and treat it as if it were your own. It also requires you to agree with the owner's parameters of sanctioned use. If I give you a hammer and tell you to hang a picture on the wall in my living room, my intention is for you to use the hammer to do what I instructed. I did not give it to you to disregard my instructions regarding what to do to my stuff, with my stuff. In the same way, God has entrusted the dance.

Thus we, as dancers, must divorce ourselves from the perception that dancer is all we are. Yes we dance, which makes us a dancer in the functional sense, but we are more than a dancer in His purpose. We are stewards of the dance. As stewards, we acknowledge that there is something bigger than the dance, beyond the dance, and yet including the dance, that we have been enlisted to exercise care over. Our dance activity is connected to a higher principle and purpose. We must be presented in our stewardship of the dance.

Being presented in our service is a choice that influences how we obey. In ministry, we place ourselves at the disposal of God. We acknowledge His providence over this gift of dance within us. We come into agreement with His determinations about how our ministry is to be structured and run, what songs we do, what engagements we accept and refuse, the choreography we do, the garments we wear, the instruments we use, who is responsible for what within the ministry, how they get into the ministry, what happens in our rehearsals, how we prepare for ministry, etc.

Substance, Form, and Result.

Throughout this chapter we have touched on the distinction between the dance and the ministry. Our ministry, the way we serve, is to seek his voice and obey what we've heard. That obedience takes on a particular form (like the dance) and produces a particular result (like healing); but obedience, the form it takes, and what it produces are three distinct elements. Dance minister, preacher, prophet, evangelist, singer, the laying on of hands, prophesying- these are not the ministry. These are vocational and physical representations that clarify the way our obedience is carried out or the form of expression that it takes on. Through this distinction I am pointing out that *anyone* can arbitrarily carry on the activities of any of these functions (stand before people and speak, grab a mic and sing, or put their hand on someone's forehead) and nothing would result from it because the form is not the ministry and the ministry is not the form. God may tell a preacher to grab a mic and sing. He may tell a singer to lay her hands on a woman's stomach and prophesy, or a dancer to preach.

Titles that we carry in ministerial positions can become confusing when we begin to think that the position itself is the ministry. We have wrongly concluded that the title of ministerial positions (i.e. "preacher") is what we are destined to become. We are sons and kings. Ministry is to be what we *do*, not who we are. Yes, God calls us to certain functions, but the substance, the individual actions that make up those functions are to be acts of obedience. For instance, God calls Bro. Macy to be a Pastor (position). His activities in the function of a Pastor should be acts of obedience, meaning he must obey God in how to prepare to deliver the word, what word to declare and when to declare it, how to set up the house God has given him to steward, and how to run the services. If Bro. Macy were to try to do any of those things outside of the realm of obedience, outside of God's prescribed manner for *him* to engage in the function of a Pastor, his actions would be fruitless because the mere activities of a ministerial position cannot persist in themselves. They only give form and tangibility to the obedience.

Now, we must further understand that the obedience is not what manifests the presence and power of God. He does that by Himself. Instead, our obedience aligns us with the flow of His power. Think about the powering of a fan. On a fan you have the cage, the blades, the on/off switch, and the power cord, which has at its end a plug and two metal prongs. When I plug the fan into the wall, is it the plug that powers the appliance? Is it the on/off switch? Or is it something else?

Inside the wall, behind the drywall and insulation, electricity is being provided into your house from an outside source so that whatever you plug into the wall will be powered. Basically, it is that electricity that is powering the fan. The metal prongs at the end of the cord are called conductors and they serve as conduits for the electricity, as electricity will only flow through certain channels. If there were wood prongs on the plug, electricity would not flow to the fan, even though it has been plugged into the electrical outlet. In the same manner, God's power only flows through a certain conduit, that being our obedience. When we obey God in the dance our dance is like the power cord, and our obedience like the metal prongs at the end of the plug. Our obedience causes us to tap into the power of the heavenlies and the electric current of God's power attaches itself to our act of obedience, flows down through our dance, and electrifies the atmosphere to produce all manner of manifestations of God's power. Our obedience is the way that we tap into the power already present in our midst, like the plug is the way to tap into the electricity that already exists in the wall to power the fan.

Another way to picture the response to our obedience is to look at a 3-ring binder. Our obedience creates alignment and an unobstructed pathway for His power to move through. Have you ever tried to put paper on the rings when the holes were not lined up? It doesn't work, right? What obedience does is align the holes with the rings (the power of God) so that they can flow through. If the holes are out of alignment, a blockage is created and only if you adjust the paper and align the holes, or tear a new hole that is aligned with the rings, can the rings go through. When our activity is aligned with the Spirit, resulting from our obedience, the power of God can flow through us and results are produced, like healing, miracles, deliverance, divine information and direction. These again are not *our* ministry, but they are the evidence that we have engaged in ministry, that we have heard and obeyed God. Healing, miracles, deliverance, divine information and direction are actually part of *God's* ministry to His people.

Authorship vs. Instrumentality

Though we stand before the people of God, *we* are not ministering to them, even though we are there for them and are addressing them. We have an assignment and responsibility to them, but *we* are not the ones ministering to them. We are ministering obedience to God, providing a free and clear pathway that *He* can work through to minister to the people. I have heard this partially said before and I always disagreed, not with the statement but with the context in which it was said and understood. That we minister to God and not man has been wrongly understood as standing in front of people and engaging in personal worship, with no regard for them that are before you. That is not what I am talking about. I only make the distinction in order to highlight the importance of our obedience, which facilitates God's ministry to His people. The whole objective of our interaction with God in this regard *is* His people. Still, we are only a conduit and facilitator for the One who actually ministers to them in the form of His presence, healing, deliverance, etc.

As a church, we have over-mystified and over-complicated being used by God. The deal is simply this: if our activity is not an act of obedience, it is not ministry, regardless of how much our garments cover our body, how many churches invite our groups to dance on their program, or how many people clap and cry when we are finished. When He directs us to give to a sister, to dance a certain song, or not to dance, do we obey? If we do we are in ministry. If not, we are not. Again, religion has prepared us to think of ministry as a grand display of supposed spirituality; but true ministry is in simple obedience: in saying what He tells you to say, and only that, dancing the song He tells you to dance, refusing the invitation He tells you to refuse. It is the simple ordinary obedience. We tend to regard only what we do in front of people as ministry but ministry actually begins in the secret confines of our individual everyday lives. When we stand before the people of God, we must do *there* what is required of us in the privacy of our homes: seek God and bring our selves and actions into agreement with what He is saying. The difference between obeying God regarding our personal lives and obeying Him regarding a group of people is that the latter is obedience in a greater capacity and immediately affects a larger group of people. Still, the task and process of ministry (setting ourselves to hear and aligning ourselves with what we've heard) remain the same.

RECAP

- Dance ministry is the process of using the vehicle of dance to carry out the act of ministry.

- The dance is not our ministry. Our ministry is to attend to the Father, and align ourselves with that which He leads us to do with and through the dance.

- The dance is a vehicle that He has entrusted to us for the fulfilling of our assignment in His purpose.

- The principle of finding out what is being asked for is central to the discussion of ministry.

- God is our customer. Our business is to use our resources (gifts, talents, abilities) to provide service that is in compliance with His specifications.

- When God calls us to participate with Him in ministry, He calls us with the intention of us coming into agreement with what He is doing and setting ourselves to producing that thing.

- In ministry, we voluntarily accept our assignment and choose to walk in agreement-obedience because we respect and acknowledge that we are handling His business.

REFLECTION QUESTIONS

➤ How did this chapter inform, clarify, and/or adjust my understanding and perception of my service through dance? How does this understanding of service inform how I will approach my dancing? What do I need to adjust?

➤ Are there any areas in my ministry where I am walking in presumption, where I have not fully sought the Lord's direction?

➤ What do I do to prepare for ministry? Have I sought the Lord about any adjustments I need to make? Am I making them?

➤ What am I doing to position myself to hear God concerning the songs I minister, choreography, garments I wear, ministry opportunities, etc? Is there anything hindering my ability to do this more deliberately?

➤ Explain the distinction between the dance and the ministry. Why is it important to understand the difference?

➤ Re-read the scriptures on obeying God. What further insight was revealed in your study? How will you apply what you have learned?

➤ Share a time when your ministry made a decision that was not an act of obedience. Considering what was covered in this chapter, what would you have done differently? What actions would have remained the same?

➤ Based on what was covered in this chapter, write a prayer to God about your service to Him. Include what you desire to accomplish through Him and Him through you.

2

Place and Function

Seeing Dance Ministry in Perspective

One of the major challenges of ministry is to keep our activity in perspective. This can be especially difficult when we factor in the necessary, but consuming, administrative, logistical, and spiritual responsibilities that it involves. It is a task unto itself to remain unabsorbed into the abundance of matters that need our attention before we ever stand before the people of God. In their immediacy we, at times, find ourselves buried in their details, temporarily forgetting that the details only exist to facilitate the real task of ministry.

The Spirit of God began to deal with me some time ago about this very issue: maintaining a global perspective of ministry. By global I mean two things: first, an awareness of how the administrative and spiritual tasks serve what transpires when I stand before the people of God. Second, I am referring to how my individual activity in ministry affects the corporate body and contributes to the corporate destiny. Towards this mindset, I began to examine our function as dance ministers. Where do we fit? What is our contribution in the house of God and in the purpose of God? To answer these, I would like to start by looking at what the body of Christ is involved in and then at how the dancer is used to assist in that endeavor.

Before we begin, imagine that you are looking at planet earth through a camera in outer space. You are far enough away to be able to see earth as a whole but its details are indiscernible blotches of whites, blues, greens, and browns. Now, imagine the camera slowly panning in, with the intricate details of earth's landscape becoming clearer, until you are so close that you can only see an individual person standing on a specific corner of a specific street. That is how this chapter will flow, beginning with what our ministry efforts ultimately contribute to, and ending with the more immediate processes that help that ultimate picture happen.

When you and I stand before the people of God to minister in the dance, we are directly contributing to the progress and development of the whole body of Christ, as is true when any of God's people go forth in their assignment. Eph 4:16 (NIV) says "From him the whole body, joined and held together by every supporting ligament, grows and builds itself up in love, as each part does its work." We dance not just for ourselves or the event that we are attending. We dance to affect far beyond those sitting in front of us, reaching even to the parts of the body that we cannot see.

The Journey.

Eph 4:12-13 (NLT)
"Their responsibility is to equip God's people to do His work and build up the church, the Body of Christ, until we come to such unity in our faith and knowledge of God's son that we will be mature and full grown in the Lord, measuring up to the full stature of Christ."

The church is on a journey of evolution and development- not yet the fullness of what it is destined to be, but through the compounded efforts of its members, it is ever evolving. What is to be the culmination of our journey?

Imagine a newborn baby. Now, imagine how ridiculous it would look for that baby to have the head size and facial features of a fully grown, bearded 35-year old man. Besides looking ridiculous, the weight and disproportion of the head would be damaging to the bodily structure of the baby. It would also make it impossible to move or function because the head is too heavy to carry. This is the picture of Christ in relation to us, a still developing, disproportionate church. Col. 1:18 says that Christ is the head and we, the church collective, are the body. Eph. 4:15 says that we are to grow up into that head in all things. In all that Christ is, in all that He did, He is still only the head. But God is not after a head. He is after a body, a proportionately mature and functioning body, not a bearded baby who can't move because his head is too big.

The various facets of the Christian walk are to culminate into a mature corporate body of believers that is made up of mature individual members, who walk in and exhibit the same degree of spiritual development as Christ.

Rom. 8:29 (NKJV) says "For whom He foreknew, He also predestined to be conformed into the image of His Son, that He might be the firstborn among many brethren." By this passage, we know that our spiritual development is to take place in the context of sonship. We were predestined to share in the calling to sonship, and we were adopted into that position at salvation. However, these truths speak to a spiritual reality that was intended to produce a physical embodiment, where we would begin to walk, think, act, see, and respond as the son we became at salvation. By the same verse we know that Jesus was never designed to be the only person who walked with the authority, relationship with God, and sense of place in the world and will of God that He walked with in the earth. He was only to be the firstborn of many brethren who would walk the earth in that manner.

Basically, then, we can say that a major objective of our journey, if not the totality of it, is for the Body of Christ to think, speak, and act like a son of God to the same depth and degree that Christ did, to the end that kingdoms of this world are made the kingdoms of our Lord by sons who understand their status, position, and authority. This, beyond salvation, healing, and deliverance, is what you and I are helping to make happen when we stand before the people to minister in the dance. Though salvation, healing, and deliverance are vital, they are but steps along the pathway of a much bigger purpose.

How does this notion of sonship apply to what we do as dancers? It contextualizes our activities (what we do) and it clarifies our approach (how we get it done). In ministry, it is so important that we understand the hierarchy of the various capacities we function in. We are to be a son first, and dancer second. What does this mean for us? It means that our dance activity must be carried out in the disposition of a son. This understanding should change how we see ourselves. We tend to say "I am a worship dancer," "I am a praise dancer." But with proper understanding, we know that we are sons who worship God in dance, sons who praise God in dance, etc. With this adjustment in perspective, we acknowledge the responsibility of sonship, as God called us to this before He called us to anything else.

How does one conduct themselves like a son in the kingdom of God? In His life and ministry, Christ demonstrated how one distinctively thinks, speaks, and acts like a son.

Sonship Defined.

Romans 8:14 (NKJV)
"For as many as are led by the Spirit of God, these are sons of God."

In Luke 8 He identifies the most distinctive attribute of a son. While sitting with His disciples and discussing the parable of the sower, some people come to Him to let Him know that His mother and brothers are trying to get to Him.

Lk 8:20 (KJV)
"And it was told him by certain which said, thy mother and thy brethren
stand without, desiring to see thee. (21) And he answered and said unto
them, my mother and my brethren are these which **hear the word of God,
and do it.**" (NIV translation says "those who hear God's word and put it into
practice.")

His response is very interesting as it shows that earthly bloodline has very little to do with true sonship. What you *do* speaks more to being a son than who you are related to. In Rom. 8:29, the word son is the Greek word *huios* (Strong's *#5207*) and it speaks about "so resembling another that distinctions between the two are indiscernible."[10] In that same verse is the word image, which means "one that closely or exactly resembles another."[11] The true question is whether you share the same character and conduct, not whether you share the same DNA. This point was also made to the religious

---

[10] The New Strong's Expanded Dictionary of Bible Words
[11] www.dictionary.com

order of the day who felt they were justified and entitled because they were natural descendants of Abraham.

John 8:39 (NKJV)

"They answered and said to Him, "Abraham is our father." Jesus said to them, "If you were Abraham's children, you would do the works of Abraham.

Gal. 3:7 (AMP)

"Know *and* understand that it is [really] the people [who live] by faith who are [the true] sons of Abraham."

Jesus also showed us the disposition of a son.

Jn. 5:19 (NLT)

"Jesus replied, "I assure you, the Son can do nothing by himself. **He does only what he sees the Father doing**. Whatever the Father does, the Son also does."[12]

Jn. 8:28 (NIV)

"So Jesus said, "When you have lifted up the Son of Man, then you will know that I am the one I claim to be and that **I do nothing on my own but speak just what the Father has taught me.**"

Jn. 12:49-50 (NIV)

"For **I did not speak of my own accord, but the Father who sent me commanded me what to say and how to say it**. I know that his command leads to eternal life. So whatever I say is just what the Father has told me to say."

Jn. 14:10 (NLT)

"Don't you believe that I am in the Father and the Father is in me? **The words I say are not my own, but my Father who lives in me does his work through me.**"

---

[12] Bold emphasis in above verses mine

Through Jesus' words, we understand that a son:

1. Positions themselves to hear God's mind and instructions on a matter before they do anything,
2. Allows themselves to be led by what they've heard in action, speech, and perspective,
3. Does what they've heard as they've heard it,
4. Understands they are the image and hand of God in the earth and to the earth. People should be able to examine a son and understand more about who God is.

A son, then, is one who recognizes the providence of God and understands their place in it – leading them to *first* seek His counsel and then proceed accordingly.

Jesus also understood the implications and the scope of His relationship with God. With such statements as "...He who has seen Me, has seen the Father (Jn. 14:9)," He realized that a major way God intended for the world to get to know Him was through the lives of His children. We cannot attain Christ's level of spiritual maturity regarding sonship without acknowledging God's intense desire and intention to collaborate with us and use us as an instrument, witness, and magnet, working and displaying Himself through us to the whole scope of human life.

Operation: EDIFY

Eph. 4 speaks of the mission to edify the Body of Christ to the degree of maturity that we have just discussed. This mission seems to be laid out in a 3-step process:

1. The perfecting of the saints.

The word perfecting, synonymous with maturing, is the Greek word *katartizo* (Strong's #2675). As I studied this definition, I saw it applying to the inward man.

- *to restore and repair.* This covers everything from restoring our relationship with God through salvation, to restoring our health, finances, family relationships, emotions, etc. - to the full restoration of what God intended when He formed man in the garden in His likeness and image, blessed Him, and endowed Him with dominion.

- *to fit, to adjust, to put in order.* This speaks to the need of renewing our mind to the word and learning how to successfully walk out and apply Kingdom principles in our lives.

2. Engaging the saints in the work of ministry.

From learning how to apply Kingdom principles in our own lives, we expand into increasing dimensions of Kingdom assignment.

3. The edification of the Body of Christ.

When done with understanding, our dancing is more than the 5-10 minutes we spend in front of the people. It is more than trying to make them feel good, and even more than trying to get them healed or saved. When we dance in purpose we impact the progress of the body of Christ. Eph. 4 shows us that this 3-step process is fulfilled through the interaction between the office and the saint.

So far in this chapter we have looked at the context that the dancer works in macrocosmically (the big picture). Now, we are panning the camera in so that we are close enough to see buildings. We are now looking at where the dancer fits within the operations inside the church building.

Eph. 4:11-12 (NKJV)
"And He Himself gave some to be apostles, some prophets, some evangelists and some pastors and teachers, for the equipping of the saints for the work of ministry, for the edifying of the body of Christ."

Eph. 4:11-12 seems to lay forth a sort of division of labor among the apostles, prophets, evangelists, pastors, teachers, and saints. The division of labor is "the breakdown of work into its tasks or parts and assigned to various people, groups, or machines for the purposes of efficiency."[13] This means that both those in the pulpit and in the pew have work to do, work of the **same** purpose that has simply been broken into parts. Both of these have responsibilities to fulfill that lead to producing strong individual members

---

[13] www.dictionary.com

who will collectively make up a proportionately mature body. The offices, consisting of the apostle, prophet, evangelist, pastor and teacher, are responsible for equipping the saints. The saints are responsible for applying their equipment to the work of ministry, or service. Along with dividing the workload among us, a system has been established for how our various groups are to work with each other. We can learn about this system by examining the interaction between the Aaronic and Levitical priesthood.

The Aaronic Priesthood

In Ex. 28:1 God commands Moses to take Aaron and his sons from among the children of Israel in order to minister to Him in the office of a priest. Aaron was ordained as the High Priest, a foreshadowing of Jesus, who would become our High Priest. One of Aaron's duties was to make atonement for his sins and those of the children of Israel. Since Jesus, it is no longer necessary for priests to make atonement for sins because He became the atonement for all sin once and for all and forever. Still, examining Aaron's other priestly duties gives insight into the responsibilities of those in the Eph 4:11 offices.

In the same chapter God gives Moses explicit instructions and details for the making of Aaron's garments. These details give us insight into the priests' and New Covenant offices' function and responsibility.

Ex. 28:11-12 (KJV)
"With the work of the engraver in stone, like the engravings of a signet, shalt thou engrave the two stones with the names of Israel: thou shalt make them to be set in ouches of gold, (12) And thou shalt put the two stones upon the shoulders of the ephod for stones of memorial unto the children of Israel: and Aaron shall bear their names before the Lord upon his two shoulders for a memorial."

One of the instructions for Aaron's garment was that a stone was to be put on each shoulder of the ephod. The names of the twelve tribes of Israel were engraved in the stones, six names in each stone. In the Hebrew culture it was understood that the name of a person revealed and determined their nature, character, authority and/or position. The verse also says that these stones served as a memorial for the children of Israel and for God.

"Memorial" is the Hebrew word *zikrown*[14], which is "a mark, so as to be remembered." Why did God want the children of Israel's names memorialized?

The children of Israel were set apart by God as His chosen people. That designation came with a certain status, as well as certain rights, privileges, and responsibilities before Him, and before other people. Their names upon the shoulders of Aaron's ephod served to evoke awareness in them of who they were, the chosen people of God, and to remind them, therefore, to conduct themselves appropriately to their position. It served to maintain that same awareness in God, which would affect how He dealt with them. Because they were His chosen people, He dealt with them, and expected them to conduct themselves, in a way very different than people carrying a different name.

In the New Covenant, Jesus and the blood serve as the memorial of who the church is before God. The Bible says that Jesus is our intermediary making intercession for us before the Father. When the Father sees the blood upon us, He acts toward us in a very definitive way. Still, we on earth must stay aware of our position and responsibility also. The offices' function is to complement and facilitate our learning about who we are in Christ and what is entitled to us (by way of rights, privileges, authority, and access), as well as what is expected of us as a result of that position.

Ex. 28:29-30 (KJV)
"And Aaron shall bear the names of the children of Israel in the breastplate of judgment upon his heart, when he goeth in unto the holy place, for a memorial before the Lord continually (30)…and Aaron shall bear the judgment of the children of Israel upon his heart before the Lord continually."

Ex. 28:36, 38 (KJV)
"And thou shalt make a plate of pure gold, and grave upon it, like the engravings of a signet, HOLINESS TO THE LORD. (38) And it shall be upon Aaron's forehead, that Aaron may bear the iniquity of the holy things,

---

[14] Strong's #2146

which the children of Israel shall hallow in all their holy gifts; and it shall be always upon his forehead, that they may be accepted before the Lord."

In both Ex. 28:29-30, 36, and 38, we see that Aaron's responsibility played a factor in how God dealt with and responded to the children of Israel. The difference between Aaron and the Eph. 4:11 offices is that Aaron was responsible for the spiritual state of the children of Israel. Jesus has fulfilled that responsibility. Now, the offices are not so much responsible for the people's spiritual state anymore, but more for the state of their spiritual walk. The nature of their responsibility is to ensure that the people have the knowledge needed to progress and mature.

Eph. 4:12 coins this responsibility as the "equipping of the saints." Webster's Unabridged Dictionary defines "equip" as:

- *To provide with what is necessary, useful, or appropriate*
- *To make ready or competent for service or action*

The offices equip the saints in two strategic ways: through feeding and through covering. In John 21:15-17 (KJV), Jesus has an exchange with His disciple Simon Peter in which He asks Simon if he loves Him three times. Each time Simon responds "Yes." Twice Jesus replies "Feed My sheep," (vrs. 16, 17) and once He replies "Feed my lambs," (vs. 15). I studied these three verses and found that sheep and lambs are the same animal; but a lamb is a baby sheep. Further, the word "feed" used in verses 15 and 17 is a different Greek word than that used in 16. "Feed" in verses 15 and 17 is the Greek word *bosko,*[15] which is to pasture (feed and nourish) or to fodder (feed). In verse 16, the Greek word *poimaino*[16] is used, which means to shepherd or supervise.

What is revealed in the exchange between Jesus and Simon, who operates as an Eph. 4:11 office, is that part of their responsibility is to feed and nourish the people. According to Eph. 4:13, the body matures through regularly feeding on faith and the knowledge of the son of God. The faith includes the premise and basis of our faith, how to exercise and live a life of faith, and what results from the use of faith. The knowledge of the son of God speaks to intellectually and experientially knowing the Son of God manifested both as Jesus, the man, and as the Word. Knowing the Son

---

[15] Strong's #*1006*
[16] Strong's #*4165*

intellectually means knowing the word and understanding the type of person Jesus was, how He thought, how He acted and reacted in life's situations. Knowing the son experientially means that you *do* the word and have contact and interaction with the spirit of God; but it also means knowing Jesus empathetically, understanding who He is because you have done what He has done.

Simon's other responsibility was to shepherd or supervise as the people applied the information and matured in the faith. As a shepherd, the office provides a covering for the people of God. Under this corporate covering, the environment surrounding the people of God is fertile, favorable, and responsive as they go to the work of ministry and go out to pursue God's will for their lives. To cover[17] is to:

- To station oneself so as to receive a throw to;

The offices specifically position themselves to receive divine information, instruction, and direction for the people of God.

- Guard the safety and further the success of one by aggressive action precluding attack;

They then bring the information to the people of God which, when cooperated with, advances the people in their walk and helps them avoid attack and pitfalls intended by the enemy.

- To maintain a check on by patrolling and watching.

Now, at this point you may be wondering why I took the time to go through all of that information. The reason is because our system of working together has designated us to assist the office in their function in the house of God and we cannot be of maximum assistance if we do not know what they are involved in. Look at Num. 3:6-9.

The Levites.

Numbers 3:6-9 (AMP)

" Bring the tribe of Levi near and set them before Aaron the priest, that they may minister to him. (NLT says "serve as his assistants.")   And they shall carry out his instructions and the duties connected with the whole assembly

---

[17] Webster's Unabridged Dictionary

before the Tent of Meeting, doing the service of the tabernacle. And they shall keep all the instruments and furnishings of the Tent of Meeting and take charge of [attending] the Israelites, to serve in the tabernacle. And you shall give the Levites [as servants and helpers] to Aaron and his sons; they are wholly given to him from among the Israelites." (NLT adds "to serve as their assistants.")

The Levites are a parallel to the saints in Eph. 4:11, which defines their responsibility as performing the "work of ministry." When studied in conjunction with Numbers, we see that when the saints perform "the work of ministry" in the house, that work is purposed to help the office fulfill their responsibility to feed and cover the people of God. As ministers, we sometimes like to get super-spiritual

Every time we go somewhere to minister, we are stepping into someone else's assignment and we are there to pour into that assignment

and claim that we serve God and not man. However, our service to God, as God Himself has ordained it, is to help those in the "office" position. How does this apply to the dancer?

The saints are equipped and matured mainly by the preaching, teaching, and application of the word. If the office's responsibility is to equip the saints, the dancer is there to reinforce and facilitate the office's efforts as they feed and cover the people. This reinforcing and facilitating comes through our movements and the songs we minister. We serve as a reinforcer when the words of our song echo what is being declared from the pulpit. For instance, if healing is being preached in the house, then our songs should include those about healing.

We serve as a facilitator when we help create a space for the equipping to occur, by creating a welcoming atmosphere for the presence of God and by readying the individual heart to receive the presence and ministry of God. When reinforcing or facilitating, the dancer becomes a vital part of helping the office in their charge to equip the saints.

You may be asking: what if my ministry is not housed in a church? What if I travel to different churches? What if I only minister at conferences, concerts, or other events? If you minister in your own self-produced events, then you are in your own assignment. Otherwise, the principle remains the same. Every time we go somewhere to minister, we are stepping into someone else's assignment and we are there to pour into that assignment. Being led by the Spirit again becomes so important because He may use us to reinforce or confirm a teaching that we weren't present for. He may use us to lay foundation for a truth that is about to be disclosed that we are not necessarily privy to, but only know what the Voice led us to do in that place. I have had many experiences where pastors and others would come to me and say *I was just teaching that* or *that was the perfect entry for what I taught today.* No matter where we go, we must realize we are entering into someone else's assignment and we've been sent there to minister into that assignment through reinforcing, facilitating, and/or preparing.

RECAP

- We must stay mindful to keep administrative and logistical responsibilities in service to our true ministry.

- We must stay mindful that our individual activity in ministry affects the corporate body and contributes to the corporate destiny.

- As a dance minister, you are contributing to the body of Christ thinking, speaking, and acting like a son of God to the same depth and degree as Christ did.

- As a dancer in the house, our job is to reinforce and enable the office in their responsibility to feed and equip the people.

- Our dance activity must be carried out in the disposition of a son.

- We must stay mindful that when we go forth in ministry through dance, we are entering into someone else's assignment and we have been sent there to minister into that assignment through reinforcing, facilitating, and/or preparing.

- We serve as a reinforcer when the words of our song and our movements echo what is being declared from the pulpit.

- We serve as a facilitator when we help create a space for the equipping to occur; by creating a welcoming atmosphere for the presence of God, and by readying the individual heart to receive the presence and ministry of God.

REFLECTION QUESTIONS

➢ How has this chapter informed, clarified, and/or adjusted my understanding and perception of my service through dance and its place in the will and purpose of God?

➢ Is there anything I am involved in or taking on that is affecting my ability to maintain a global perspective about what I do in ministry through dance?

➢ Understanding my place in the big picture, and understanding what is affected by my activity in ministry, are there things that I need to shift, pick back up, adjust, remove, etc?

➢ What are the logistical and administrative responsibilities involved in my ministry? Have I sought the Lord in how to address these? Have I allowed any of them to consume my time in a way that hinders me from communing with God as I should? What do I need to adjust (through delegating, removing, etc)?

➢ What must I consider when preparing to minister into someone else's assignment?

➢ Am I handling all aspects of my ministry with the disposition of a son? In what ways do I need to adjust?

➢ Why is the 3-step process of Eph. 4 so important to our understanding of ministry? Why is it important to understand our place within that? How does understanding this process change or shift how you conduct ministry?

➢ Based on what was covered in this chapter, write a prayer to God about your place in His operation. Include what you desire to accomplish through Him and Him through you.

3
The Effectiveness of Dance Ministry

Dance ministry is presented through the elements of song (instrumentation and the word) and movement. Both song and movement have specific and strategic qualities that help us fulfill our function. They also provide another medium for visualizing and understanding the word of God.

At the end of the previous chapter, we began to establish that the dance minister, in the context of the local church, functions in several ways:

1. They help the office equip the saints.
2. In this capacity, the dancer is a reinforcement agent and a facilitator.
3. The dancer reinforces and facilitates the equipping process through the songs they minister and their movement.

In this chapter, we will delve deeper into these functions, panning our camera in even closer until an individual face fills our lens. Until now, we have been looking at the context and environment in which dance ministry operates. We will now look at the vehicle itself, as a whole and in its parts.

So far we know:

1. The body of Christ is on a journey to mature spiritually.
2. This spiritual maturity comes by learning and applying what we learn about the word of God and faith. (Eph. 4)
3. The relationship between office and saint is a way the learning and application of faith and God's word is initiated and nurtured. (Eph 4:11-12)

The Absence of Cling

Spiritual maturity comes by learning, and then *applying* what we have learned. In our present church system, we have put much focus and energy into acquiring knowledge about the word of God. With new churches forming every month, CD's and DVD's, seminaries and Christian colleges, Christian bookstores, 24-hour Christian television, podcasts, radio, and internet streaming, there is more access to instruction about the word of God now than has ever existed in the history of mankind. We know a lot of information about the word of God. And yet, there remains an overwhelming imbalance between the mass of information that we have acquired, and the implementation of that information in the way we live our lives and the fruit it should be producing.

Church in many buildings now consists of a café culture with audiences coming in, singing, sitting down to listen to a speaker for an hour, and returning to their life as usual. There is a loss of the sense that we have a responsibility and opportunity to participate; that what we have just listened to demands a response and requires action. The *going* to church seems to have become the focus, not the life application of what we learn there. Despite the fact that we go to church Sunday after Sunday, *and* Wednesday, Friday, and Saturday; despite the fact that we watch TBN and buy messages, nothing significant ever seems to change in what emanates from the church as a collective body. Individuals progress. Individuals make life changes. But there are so few examples of greater numbers being conspicuously affected by contact with this God so full of power to produce change in and through us.

There is a reason for this.

The reason is because as we hear and learn, we have a responsibility to participate, to respond and to react, as we are in relationship with both a living God and a living Word. I sincerely believe that our current imbalance has much to do with the fact that we have become disconnected with how to participate with God's word in the way that produces change. We are apathetic to the fact that there is such a thing as dead faith, or a state of being where we believe with all our heart, yet experience impotence.

We have established that we are quite knowledgeable of what the word says, but how are we to interact with it? How are we to **live** with it? Hab. 2:4 tells us that the just shall live by faith. James tells us that faith requires action, and will produce nothing until action that corresponds with what we believe takes place.

James 2:17-24 (AMP)

So also faith, if it does not have works (deeds and actions of obedience to back it up), by itself is destitute of power (inoperative, dead). But someone will say [to you then], You [say you] have faith, and I have [good] works. Now you show me your [alleged] faith apart from any [good] works [if you can], and I by [good] works [of obedience] will show you my faith. You believe that God is one; you do well. So do the demons believe and shudder [in terror and horror such as make a man's hair stand on end and contract the surface of his skin]! Are you willing to be shown [proof], you foolish (unproductive, spiritually deficient) fellow, that faith apart from [good] works is inactive and ineffective and worthless? Was not our forefather Abraham [shown to be] justified (made acceptable to God) by [his] works when he brought to the altar as an offering his [own] son Isaac? You see that [his] faith was cooperating with his works, and [his] faith was completed and reached its supreme expression [when he implemented it] by [good] works. And [so] the Scripture was fulfilled that says, Abraham believed in (adhered to, trusted in, and relied on) God, and this was accounted to him as righteousness (as conformity to God's will in thought and deed), and he was called God's friend. You see that a man is justified (pronounced righteous before God) through what he does and not alone through faith [through works of obedience as well as by what he believes]." (emphasis mine)

An incomplete understanding of faith has left many of us thinking that it is simply about believing. Believing, by itself, is a static and temporary state of being that *will* lose vigor over time if it is not put to use. Belief is simply "the reason to," the goad that pricks us, if only by desire, to move into action towards our belief.

Rom. 10:17 tells us that faith comes by hearing, and hearing by the word of God. When we hear God's word and its potent truth hits our spirit, a flame is ignited within us, hope springs within us, belief in that word is created. However, that initial state of belief is vacillating, and not yet rooted in our hearts. Lk 8: 11-14 (NLT) illustrates the cause of this vacillation:

"This is the meaning of the story: The seed is God's message. The seed that fell on the hard path represents those who hear the message, but then the Devil comes and steals it away and prevents them from believing and being saved. The rocky soil represents those who hear the message with joy. But like young plants in such soil, their roots don't go very deep. They believe for a while, but they wilt when the hot winds of testing blow. The thorny ground represents those who hear and accept the message, but all too quickly the message is crowded out by the cares and riches and pleasures of this life. And so they never grow into maturity. **But the good soil represents** *honest, good-hearted* **people who hear God's message, cling to it, and steadily produce a huge harvest.** *"*(emphasis mine)

If you notice, all four of these examples heard the word, like we hear the word. The issue in our Christian walk is not the access to information. People *are* hearing the word. Yet, only one of the Luke 8 hearers produced anything. Why? Rom. 10:17 says that faith (believing a matter is so true that you do something about it) comes by hearing. I looked up the word "come" and one of its definitions was "to germinate," which means "to begin to grow or develop; to produce; to cause to come into existence." When we hear God's word, we are also supposed to, at some point, be living in the manifested reality of that word. The word of God was never meant to be something we only read in a book, but instead it is to be a telling of what is, and is about to manifest in our lives. The other thing I noticed about this verse is that it says that faith grows and produces through the process of hear-"ing." The "-ing" suffix creates a present participle form of the verb "hear." Present participles denote "repetition or duration of an activity or event."[18] One of the reasons we find our faith is so vacillating is because on Sunday we "heard," but during the week, we are not hear-"ing." Unless you are in an environment that emphasizes this, the critical importance of hear-"ing" beyond Sunday is not being stressed.

Now, there is a channel of hear-"ing" that is even more potent than hearing the word preached on Sunday, or listening to it from a tape or television program on Tuesday. There is a way of hear-"ing" God's word that is more powerful than hearing it from any other outside source.

Mt. 21:21 (NKJV)
"So Jesus answered and said to them, "Assuredly, I say to you, if you have faith and do not doubt, you will not only do what was done to the fig tree, but also if **you say** to this mountain, 'Be removed and be cast into the sea,' it will be done." (emphasis mine)

Mk. 11:23 (NKJV)
"For assuredly, I say to you, **whoever [them self] says** to this mountain, 'Be removed and be cast into the sea,' and does not doubt in his heart, but believes that those things he says will be done, he will have whatever he says." (emphasis mine)

Our tendency, at least mine was, when we read these verses is to focus on the "believe-and-not-doubt" aspect of them. However, there is more instruction there on the action to be taken. Faith without works will not produce. Believing something and not taking any action in line with that belief will produce nothing.

The fundamental and consistent action we are to take once belief is ignited in our hearts is to SPEAK it. We were created in the image and likeness of a speaking God who speaks His world into existence. The most powerful and fruit-producing method for hear-"ing" is by hearing *ourselves* speak. The Bible is loaded with verses about the need for care with our speech because we were created to operate like our God who speaks things

---

[18] www.dictionary.com

into existence. James instructs us of the magnificent effect of this seemingly insignificant act.

James 3:2-5 (AMP)

"For we all often stumble and fall and offend in many things. And if anyone does not offend in speech [never says the wrong things], he is a fully developed character and a perfect man, able to control his whole body and to curb his entire nature. If we set bits in the horses' mouths to make them obey us, we can turn their whole bodies about. Likewise, look at the ships: though they are so great and are driven by rough winds, they are steered by a very small rudder wherever the impulse of the helmsman determines. Even so the tongue is a little member, and it can boast of great things. See how much wood or how great a forest a tiny spark can set ablaze!"

The powerful truth revealed in this passage is that our whole body, environment and circumstance are affected by what comes out of our mouth. WHOA! The will, the mind, the emotions, and the metaphysical atmosphere around us respond to what we say. Contextualizing this, then, the goal for us, as individuals and as a corporate body, is to mature spiritually and produce fruit that evinces that maturity amidst a watching and waiting world. By Eph 4, we know that comes by proper interaction with faith and the knowledge of the Son of God, where we begin to put to work what we have been learning. The foundational way we are to apply what we learn is to speak what we learn, and more so, to make it a part of the *way* we talk. Once it becomes a part of the way we talk, we will begin to see something very different as our mind, will and actions begin to align themselves with our confession. The question then becomes if it is that easy, why is it not happening with the frequency that it should? I had to ask myself the same question. Why have I not been doing this consistently, when I know to do it and I intend to do it? Truthfully, the answer lies much in the same reasons that Lk. 8:11-14 laid forth. Have you ever heard a message that rocked your spirit at its core, and as you sat there you vowed to not let this word passively slip away into nothingness, but when you got home, that fire seemed to have all but quenched? Perhaps you forgot what was preached. Perhaps you remembered but got distracted by very real situations. The reality is that there are very real threats to the seed sown in the hearts of the people of God, and if they are ever going to have a chance to make that seed produce, there must be a mechanism in place to help the people stay connected to the word long enough for belief to become action and manifestation to occur. Again, our issue is not dissemination, it is longevity of connection. Lk. 8 showed that the fourth example produced because it *clung* to the word. Understanding this context, let's now look at the vehicle of dance ministry.

SONG

Years ago, the Spirit of God began to deal with me about song. He instructed that it has a specific use and strategy. I found this interesting because I never thought of song as having a strategy. I knew that song was an integral part of what I did, I knew it was important to pray and be led to the song I would minister as it was the word of God for that occasion, and I knew to study the words of the song; but I never gave thought to its strategic use. As I began to study it, though, I discovered *why* those things I knew to do were so important.

The Allure of Song.

There is something about music that remains etched in our minds forever. Once we commit a song to memory, no matter how absent it may be from our lives, it remains unforgettable in our minds. It is ageless and limitless. It transcends all conceivable barriers, discriminating or excluding no one. There is not a person on earth that remains unaffected by its existence. Music lasts long beyond its creation and targeted time period, always spilling into populations other than those for whom it was created.

Most interesting is how much about music we remember. There are songs that I hear on the radio, or that just pop into my head that I haven't heard in years, and yet still remember like I heard it a few minutes ago. It is not just the words I remember either. I remember every high note, every run, the melody, instrumentation and quirky articulation of the lyrics. I remember all my favorite parts that made me want to play the whole song over and over again.

Music, especially that from previous times in our lives, always comes with some degree of nostalgia. We don't just remember the words and beats and specific ways of singing the lyrics, but we remember where we were when we were most connected to it: the feeling it gave us, our state of mind, what was going on in our lives, who was in our lives, moments of clarity, etc.

More than anything though, music is just plain fun!! It affects us emotionally and psychologically. We love to listen to it and sing at the top of our lungs even though we sound horrible. We'll even listen to and sing songs with messages we don't necessarily agree with if they have a great sound. Music helps make harsh truths easier to accept. Because of all these wonderful qualities of music, we sing, and we sing all the time, the same song over and over again. Even songs that we hate, we find that we can't get them out of our head. I believe that God created all these alluring attributes in music, and in His infinite wisdom, employs them for the assurance of the effective distribution and remaining of His word.

In Deut. 31:19-21 (KJV), we are shown a poignant example of this truth.

> "Now therefore write ye this song for you, and <u>teach</u> it to the children of Israel: <u>put</u> it in their <u>mouths</u>, that this song may be a <u>witness</u> for me against the children of Israel. For when I shall have brought them into the land which I sware unto their fathers, that floweth with milk and honey; and they shall have eaten and filled themselves, and waxen fat; then they will turn unto other gods, and serve them, and provoke me, and break my covenant. And it shall come to pass, when many evils and troubles are befallen them, that this song shall <u>testify</u> against them as a witness; for it shall not be <u>forgotten</u> out of the mouths of their seed..."

The children of Israel are about to cross over into the land that God has promised them. Moses was disobedient and would therefore not be allowed to cross over with them. In his place Joshua would lead Israel into the land.

Before Moses dies, God foretells Israel's rebellion, how He will deal with them in response and how they can restore themselves.

After He gives this information to Moses, notice what He tells Moses to do with it: "Now therefore write ye this song for you, and teach it to the children of Israel: put it in their mouths, that this song may be a witness for me against the children of Israel." I always found this interesting. Instead of telling Moses to simply read, or preach it, or put it in a memo and distribute it to them, he specifically commands Moses to put the information into a song. As I studied this passage, God showed me song's strategy.

1. It keeps us consciously connected to the word.

People won't speak or obey what they don't remember or what is removed from their immediate cognizance. Once the word is declared, the song in the dancer's ministry helps the people stay consciously connected to the word. We find out how through closer examination into God's instructions to Moses.

Teach: #3925 (lamad): to goad
Put: to set or make as a sign
Sign: a conspicuously placed word or legend of direction, warning,
   identification or other information of general concern. (WUD)[1]
Mouths: #6310 (peh): speech, sentence
Witness: #5707 (ed): recorder, testify by reiteration, duplicate or repeat
Testify: #6030 (anah): respond to; to begin to speak
Forgotten: #7911 (shakach): to mislay (put in an unremembered place[1])

God tells Moses to teach the song to the children of Israel, by putting it in their mouths. At first this seems insignificant but referring to the definitions reveals its importance. The word "teach" is to goad, which is to prod, urge or stimulate to motion.[19] Song is an aural stimulus that by nature pulls our attention. When a song enters our consciousness, it is to our spirit what a big orange sign is to our eyes. As long as it is in our periphery it draws our focus. Very rarely does a song come into our head, play one time, and leave. Instead, it is like a child who incessantly pulls at you until you

---

[19] www.dictionary.com

acknowledge and interact with them. Until you've sang the words of that nagging song a few times, it will not leave you alone.

In teaching the song containing God's word to Israel, the aural stimulation of the song would continue to draw Israel's attention. Moses was also told to put the song in their mouths. This immediately seems to be restating the obvious. Of course you would put the words in their mouth if you were teaching them the song. Why the distinction?

Teaching the song was a means of getting their attention. Putting the song in their mouth was a way of applying their attention, once had. Moses' instructions to put the song in Israel's mouth actually meant to make it a part of their everyday conversation. If you refer back to the passage we discussed in James, you can remember how powerful words are in influencing the human spirit.

"Put" is defined as making or setting as a sign. A sign is a conspicuously placed word or legend of direction, warning, identification or other information of general concern.[20] Signs are sources of information that are strategically designed and located to draw attention. They are always placed where they are plainly visible and easily accessible. Dt. 30:11, 14 (KJV) says "For this commandment which I command thee this day, it is not hidden from thee, neither is it afar off...But the word is nigh thee in thy mouth and in thy heart, that thou mayest do it." In order to do the word, you must be near the word. Song is a big splotch of orange that keeps pulling our focus to the sign in our mouth- the word, and its incessant stimulation causes our focus to remain on the word.

If you refer back to the parable of the sower in Lk. 8, you will remember that all four examples had the same opportunity to hear the same word; however, it did not produce the same result in them all. The difference between the first three and the last was the longevity of the connection they had to the word. For various reasons the first three lost contact with the word before it produced in their lives, whereas the fourth hearer kept, or stayed near, the word (*katecho in Greek: to keep firm possession of, to keep in the mind or memory*). He maintained a close connection to the word for the time it took to materialize.

---

[20] Webster's Unabridged Dictionary

This is where song helps. It is a strategic instrument designed to ensure the remaining of God's word in the consciousness of His people. It is not enough to simply hear or know the word. You can know the word but never apply it because it is out of mind. The offices give the word, but there must be a mechanism in place to help the people stay connected to the word long enough for faith to become action, and for action to bring about manifestation. Song is one of those mechanisms. The fact is we *will* sing the songs that come up into our spirit. Our tendency to sing the same song over and over again makes song a perfect instrument to ensure a consistent conscious connection to the word. If the lyrics are the word of God, by singing the song, we are speaking the word.

2. It ensures the remembrance of the word.

Deut 31:19 (KJV)
"Now therefore write ye this song for you, and teach it to the children of Israel: put it in their mouths, <u>that this song may be a witness for me against the children of Israel.</u>
(emphasis mine)

> *There must be a mechanism in place to help the people stay connected to the word long enough for belief to become action and manifestation to occur*

The word "witness" is the Hebrew word *ed* (Strong's #5707), which is a recorder. It means to repeat and reiterate. A recorder is a device that captures an image and/or what has been said and plays it back, exactly how it happened. The Holy Spirit promised that He would bring back to our remembrance all He has said to us,[21] that He would suggest it to our memory, recall it in our mind, and cause us to remember.[22] I sincerely believe that song is one of the devices He uses to fulfill that promise.

In Deut. 31:21, God says that the song "will not be forgotten out of the mouths of their seed..." "Forgotten" is the Hebrew word *shakach,* to put in

---

[21] John 14:26
[22] Strong's Exhaustive Concordance

an unremembered place.[23]   The potency of that song would have such remaining power that their great-grandchildren would still be singing it and talking about it. Song is so effective in disseminating and prolonging the awareness of information that many indigenous people used this method of oral history to pass down customs, knowledge, and tradition to the next generation. Think about the lineage of many of the hymns we still sing in church today.

Because we never forget the words of songs, when we put God's word into song it helps us remember, stand on, and apply the word of God. The strategy, then, is that the word is declared, capsulated into song, and given to the people of God. During the week the song plays in their spirit over and over like a tape recorder. As they continue to hear and sing the song, its words embed and fortify themselves more in their heart. Out of the abundance of their heart their mouth begins to speak. As they speak, their mind and thoughts begin to cooperate with what is coming out of their mouth and they begin to act accordingly as revelation and instruction bud from the seed of that word sown. For this reason, the praise and worship ministry must be attentive to what is being declared over the pulpit because it is our job to reinforce the offices' efforts to help the people stay connected to the word long enough for it to produce fruit in their lives. Song is a part of the way we accomplish that.

Exposing the Point of Access.

Besides reinforcing the word spoken in their songs, the dance minister also serves as a facilitator, through the function of a praise and worship leader.

When the people come into the house of God, they are just getting out of traffic, coming from a contentious home environment, dealing with work, family, health, financial, and marital issues. All of these issues consume the mind and thoughts and, if not confronted, make it difficult, if not impossible for the word of God to take root in their heart. Lk. 8:14 speaks to the dangers of such anxieties, explaining that they choke out the effectiveness of the word, crowding the mind so that nothing else can get in or be heard above their overwhelming presence.

---

[23] Strong's #7911

Ps. 100:4 (KJV) says that we are to "enter His gates with thanksgiving and His courts with praise. Courts and gates are structures surrounding a place of occupancy- whether it be a house, business, temple, etc. Gates are defined as a means of access.[24] A court is an extent of open ground partially or completely enclosed by walls or buildings.[25] In reading this verse we know that we do not literally enter His gates and courts because He has no physical place of occupancy that we are able to enter. Where, then, are these gates and courts of the Lord? Where is His place of occupancy? IN US!

1 Co. 6:19 (KJV) and 2 Co. 6:16 (KJV) tell us that our body is the temple of the living God. 2 Co. 6:16 (KJV) further says He dwells in us and walks in us. The gates and courts we are trying to get to are within ourselves.

The gates represent our means of access. The open courts represent that state of being where we are so mentally and spiritually consumed with the awareness of God's presence within us and around us, that there is no room in our thoughts or heart for anxiety, fear, or distress to enter. The openness of the court gives room to hear. There is no bombardment or overcrowding of thoughts and our attention is not divided among the various issues we face, providing a quiet and peaceful environment where we can listen. It allows us to hear God when He speaks from within us, and to hear His voice inside the voice when He speaks outside of us (e.g. preacher). The enclosing of the court provides a place of refuge. Though the issues are still there, the court enables us to separate ourselves from them in order to receive what we need to deal with them.

The anxieties and issues that we bring into the house and presence of God can literally choke out our ability to hear or feel Him. If the word of God is delivered but the people are not in the right place mentally, Lk. 8:14 occurs and our service is rendered ineffective. The way we corporately and personally get into His courts and gates is through thanksgiving and praise. Thanksgiving means we are thanking God, which puts us back in a mindset and place of remembrance of what He's done, said, and brought us through, which will encourage us in our present circumstance. Praise gets us back in tune with the bigger source, the more able source as we begin to recount His strengths, promises, and abilities. In remembering the strength and voracity of our God, we are reminded and assured of His ability to deliver us from our

---

[24] Dictionary.com
[25] Dictionary.com

present circumstance. As a praise and worship leader, we do not facilitate this time as a mere formality or act of protocol. We are helping to expose that good ground in each individual for the word to be sown into, for it is only the good ground that can retain the word once sown.

Understanding the impact of song makes it very important that we be sensitive to the leading of the Holy Spirit regarding the songs we minister. We must be like Chenaniah, discerning and perceptive.[26] This is a vital responsibility and fortunately we have several promises we can stand on to help us in it:

- "Seek his will in all you do, and he will show you which path to take." Prov 3:6 (NLT)

We are to set our heart to find out what God wants and in return He promises to show us what to do and how to get it done. It was never God's intention for us to fumble about trying to figure out how to do this alone.

- "Roll your works unto the Lord. Commit them wholly to Him and He will cause your thoughts to become agreeable to His will and your plans will be established and succeed." Prov. 16:3 (AMP)

After we have done this in faith, we can trust that the thoughts that come into our mind concerning that matter are in line with the will of God.

- "Your ears shall hear a word behind you, saying 'this is the way; walk in it.'" Isai. 30:21 (NKJV) *We now say 'within' you since we know the Spirit of God dwells on the inside of us.*

- The Father will give you what you should say and what you should speak. Jn. 12:49

Remember, we are speaking on His behalf, employed in His purpose to declare His word to His people. He will give us what to say. Our job is to simply position ourselves to hear and do what we've heard.

---

[26] 1 Chr. 15:22 Chenaniah was the chief Levite over song.

Obtaining the In-Season Song.

I used to host an online dance community where dancers would often post messages like: "Does anyone know good songs for healing?" Such resources are great in our search for songs to minister but it should not be the first step we take. The question we must first answer within ourselves is would we be satisfied to bring *a* word from God, or do we want to bring *the* word of God? There are always various songs that would be thematically appropriate for different occasions but we don't just want a song that would fit the occasion. We want to bring the word in season!

The Spirit of God gave me three prayer outlines for receiving the in-season song, as well as guidelines from the word to discern His leading. These are not meant to be prayed word for word, although you could, but they are just to get you thinking along the right track.

Ministry in your church home.
Lord, I am here to assist the man/woman of God You have placed over this house in equipping the people of God. _____ is what they are declaring and I know that my job is to be of one sound with them and reinforce Your word coming through them to the people. Holy Spirit, You are the helper. Lead me to Your song for this house. I receive and thank you for Your direction.

Ministry in other churches.
Lord, I am here to assist the man/woman of God You have placed over this house in equipping the people of God. Holy Spirit, You are the helper. Lead me to Your song for this house. I receive and thank you for Your direction.

Other.
Lord, I am here on assignment to declare Your word to Your people. What do they need to hear from You today. Lead me to the song that declares Your right now word to them. I receive and thank you for Your direction.

Once we pray in faith, God will lead us in various ways. He gave me some guidelines to discern His leading, which will be towards the following directions:

1. Songs that reiterate what the man/woman of God is declaring over the pulpit (Deut. 31:19/2 Chr. 29:30)

What comes from that pulpit is direction and information for the house. As God did with Moses, He reveals information we need for a victorious and progressive walk. It is then our responsibility to keep ourselves connected to that word and apply it. The dancer assists in this process by reinforcing what is declared through our song and movement. It is vital, then, that our ministry help the people stay connected to the word in season, the right now word, coming from the pulpit. This would mean if the man/woman of God is preaching about healing, we need to seek God for the right now song to reinforce what is being preached about healing. Though you may have an absolutely anointed, God-breathed song about prosperity, your ministry, for the time being, is needed to reinforce healing.

2. Songs that instruct in the laws, principles, and commands of God (not the ten commandments) (1 Chr. 15:22)

In this passage, "song" is the Hebrew word *massa* (Strong's #4853): "the utterance, chiefly a doom."[27] A doom is an ordinance or decree, which contains the rules, practices, and policies to be followed. This is why our praise and worship songs have an authoritative tone- "Lift your hands," "Exalt the Lord." They were used to communicate the governmental and social expectations to the people.

3. Songs that remind people of God's doing, and that thank and praise Him (1 Chr. 16:4)

At times when we are walking out our faith, we need to be reminded of what God did for us in the past to help push us through to what He is doing for us presently. We also have to remember to thank Him for past victories, as gratitude is an essential part in continuing to move forward.

4. Psalms (scripture to music), Hymns (songs based on scripture but not directly scripture), Spiritual songs (songs from the Spirit – rhema in nature) (Eph. 5:19/Col 3:16)

This helps when we are standing on specific scriptures. Song helps us remember the word declared, and keeps us conscious of it so we can apply it.

---

[27] Strong's Exhaustive Concordance

5. Songs that praise and worship God. (Jn. 4:32, 34/Heb 13:15)

"Let us now continually offer up the sacrifice of praise: that is, the fruit of our lips giving thanks to His name."

The sacrifice of praise is interesting. In the Old Covenant, the priests were required to bring sacrifices to God to maintain and be restored back to the state of righteousness, which you and I receive automatically upon salvation. Since Jesus sacrificed Himself and bore the penalty of our sins through bloodshed, there is no longer a need for a sin sacrifice of blood to be offered up. However, God still wants a sacrifice to be offered up to Him. He wants our praise, or more succinctly, the fruit of our lips (our words) giving thanks to His name. Just as the blood was poured onto the altar by the priest, we who are also priests[28] are to pour our words onto the altar of our dispensation.

Not all songs that talk to or about God are praise and worship. As we lead the people of God in this, it is important for us to understand the distinction. Heb. 13:15 gives us the biblical definition of true praise. It says "let us continually offer up the sacrifice of praise, that is...," meaning here is the definition of praise: "the fruit of our lips giving thanks to His name." "Giving thanks" is the Greek word *homologeo*,[29] meaning to say the same thing as another. True praise is when we say to or about God what He has said or revealed about Himself. While teaching about this, McClendon taught that the difference between praise and worship is the direction in which you are speaking. Praise is talking about God (He is) and worship is talking to God (You are). Still, the fundamental component of them both is the same- they must say about God what He has said or revealed about Himself, otherwise it is not praise or worship.

Song plays a very important role in dance ministry and in the Body of Christ at large. The songs we choose impact the perception and expectation people have about God and His ability to victoriously move them through, around, and over their situations. I hope that this information will move us to change the way we approach song selection and provoke us to pray that our ministry would kindle more far-reaching results. It would be good for us to pray that the songs we minister would not only get people healed and saved, but that they would also continue to admonish the people throughout

---

[28] 1 Ptr. 2:11
[29] Strong's #*3670*

the week, that the images and the way God dealt with them would continue to encouragingly bother them when they go home, and that their speaking of the word would not be a mindless regurgitation but as they sing it, that the word would begin to take root in their heart and stir up their inspiration and faith.

DANCE

The dance has been quite an issue of controversy within the church. There are disagreements on what to wear when you dance, when you can dance, what parts of your body can be moved when you dance, or whether you can dance in the church at all. My approach in addressing the role of the dance is not to tell you what different dance movements mean, how you are supposed to dance, or anything of that sort. God has dealt with me very liberally concerning this and I hope to encourage you, that you would dance with the liberty that God intended for you to have. Because there is no specific direction in the Bible concerning the dance, much room has been left for the proliferation of individual convictions as dance ministry doctrine. I intend to hopefully dispel, through the word, some of the unfounded, religious, man-imposed doctrines that we have tried to force on each other. In dealing with me, God gave me guidelines from His word to line my dance up with, and those are what I will share with you. In that, there is one absolute that He impressed upon me about the dance: to build it the way He showed it to me.

In Exodus 25:8-9 (NKJV), God commands Moses to build Him a sanctuary:

"And let them make Me a sanctuary, that I may dwell among them. According to all that I show you, that is the pattern of the tabernacle and the pattern of all its furnishings, (KJV says *instruments*) just so shall you make it."

In these two verses is found significant insight into why we build, and how we are supposed to build at His command.

A Place to Dwell with my People

In this encounter, God tells Moses that He wants a sanctuary to be built so that He may dwell among His people. It is so vitally important for us to remember that the essential purpose of our dance is for God to dwell and be enthroned among His people – not for them to get saved, healed, and delivered, etc. Once God is manifest among His people, those things will occur because they are in Him and they come with Him; but they are not the reason we do what we do. He is the reason we do what we do. It is interesting that God always wanted us to seek His face, not His hands. He encourages us to remember what His hands can do, but His desire is for us to pursue Him, the person.

Build Me a Sanctuary, and Just So shall you make it.

In our modern vernacular, we usually associate a sanctuary as being a building. However, the literal translation for "sanctuary" in this passage is "sacred place," which does not refer exclusively to a building. If you read on, God further clarifies to Moses that the sacred place is to consist of the tabernacle and all its furnishings or instruments. In the Old Covenant, sanctuaries were tabernacles and temples made with animal skins, threads, and wood. In the New Covenant, however, we are "the temple of the living God (1 Co. 6:19)." In the New Testament, specifically 2 Cor. 5:4 and 2 Pet. 1:13 and 14, when the authors used the word "tabernacle," they were actually referring to the human spirit. The sanctuary God commanded contained a tabernacle *and* all its furnishings. If the New Covenant tabernacle or temple is the human body, and more succinctly the spirit of man, then our furnishings would include our gifts, talents, and abilities, and what results from them.

The sacred place that God commands us to construct, then, could be the word of God we declare over our personal lives, or through the pulpit. It can be a song, our business, our life and relationships, or in our case, a dance. The sacred place Moses was to build had the form of a tent-like structure made with animal skins, threads, wood, etc. The sacred place we are to build takes the form of dance. If we were then to apply verses 8-9 to the dancer, it would read like this: And let them make Me a [dance], that I may dwell among them. According to all that I show you, that is the [choreography] of the [dance], and the pattern of all its [costuming, lighting, props, and sound design], just so shall you make it.

In His command to Moses, it is significant to note that God specifically said He wanted a sanctuary, or sacred place built. A sacred place is a place set apart, distinct, and holy. This means there are certain standards and specific qualifications that must be met if what we build is to qualify as a sacred place. It becomes crucial, then, that we, who want the dwelling presence of the Almighty, understand what makes what we build set apart or distinct.

God is holy[30] (qadowsh: Hebrew for "set apart, or separate"). God and His word are one and the same.[31] If God is holy, and He and His word are the same, then His word must therefore also be holy. Anything that God instructs us to build is holy because the instruction was formed out of the holy word of a holy God. When we build according to His holy word, what we have built then becomes holy, because the Author and the instructions were holy. If we construct our dance according to His instructions regarding the song we dance to, the choreography, costuming, and lighting, our dance then becomes holy, and we can rest assured that the presence of God will be manifest in our midst because a holy, or sacred place is where He promised to reside.

I want you to notice that in qualifying holiness regarding the dance, I mentioned nothing about moving my body a specific way or wearing a specific kind of garment. Garments and movements do not constitute holiness. Aligning our speech and actions with God's word to us makes what we do holy. By this, I am basically giving attention to the reality that our assignments are individual and distinct and require different things – including how we move and what we wear. What God instructs one to do, then, is not necessarily the same thing He is instructing us all to do because we have different assignments and we are sent to different kinds of people. "Holiness" is more faceted than we have attributed.

A Part of the Way He Speaks

In June 2013, I was studying to teach my choreography workshop, Unlocking Movement that Speaks, which specifically focuses on declaring

---

[30] Ps. 99:9
[31] John 1:1

the word of God through dance. As I was studying, I visited Ezekiel 4 and 5, two passages I have often visited over the years as the Lord has taught me about ministry through dance. Though I know these accounts well, when I read them this time, He showed me something I had never seen before. This time, He pointedly showed me that He uses physical movement. But more than that, He showed me that movement is a part of the way He speaks. The imagery and dramatization created by physical movement are critical and essential to the way He communicates. This blew my mind! It breathed life back into my assignment in dance. I saw my part as a dancer in a whole new light and significance.

I cannot begin to tell you how much I needed this – in a time when I was struggling to continue to see the importance of dance in ministry; when I was struggling in questioning whether I was being too deep about it, wondering if this was all we would ever see in dance ministry, questioning whether I would ever truly see that magnificent manifestation of the presence and power of God through dance that was so real and vivid in my spirit. But then He showed me this, and I believed again that dance was not just something we came up with to fill our time, make our services more lively, or give our youth something to do. In a new way He showed me that movement absolutely had a place and relevance *to Him.* I saw again that dancers were not alone in our hearts conviction that dance in God was something of value, with something to contribute in God's plan and in His execution of that plan.

In Ezek. 4 and 5, Ezek. 37:16-19, 1 Kgs. 11:30-40, 2 Kgs. 13:15-19, and Isa. 20:1-6, we see very clearly that movement and the imagery it creates are essential to the way God communicates. Each of these occasions shares several elements:

1. God directs the mover in what to do and for how long. In Ezek 12:18 and 21:6, He also directs *how* He wants the movements done, telling Ezekiel to eat his bread *with quaking* and drink his water *with trembling and with carefulness.* In chapter 21, He tells him to sigh with bitterness.

2. The movements were done so that they would be seen by the people. In Ezek. 4:3, God tells Ezekiel that the movements he is doing would be a "sign" to Israel. That word "sign" is the Hebrew

word "owth," and it refers to something whose purpose is to keep whatever is seen in the observer's memory.

3. God spoke from the movements. They were directly connected to what He was saying and they were necessary to fully communicate His intentions.

4. The movements served to demonstrate what God was saying.

5. God always revealed what the movements/dramatizations meant.

6. The movements always spoke on God's behalf, communicating His mind, feelings, and words.

7. More was being communicated than what the simple movements in themselves would justify.

This provides a perfect segue into the matter of prophetic dance.

Prophetic dance

Ezekiel was the quintessential prophetic mover. He was a prophet by office, but he is, to me, the best example for us to learn from and get a better understanding of prophetic dance. I will say at the outset that mining the deep inner workings of prophetic dance is not my grace nor my assignment. However, the Lord did direct me to address a certain small part of this matter.

I often hear this term "prophetic dance" used to represent dance that is of a spontaneous nature. Somehow, prophetic operation has become inextricably tied to spontaneity. This is easy to understand because when we see prophecy come forth, it always has the appearance of being a spontaneous action. Though it does occur spontaneously at times, this is not always the case. If you study the delivery of prophecy in the Bible, you will see that what qualifies something as prophetic is whether it was inspired from the mouth of God. That being the case, if our dance is done as Ezekiel said, *as we were commanded,* then we are all operating in a manner of the prophetic, though we may not be operating in the office of a prophet. It is not our job, though, to try to determine whether people are moving in the prophetic or flowing spontaneously of their own accord; but by the time they finish, we will know.

Further, just as there were times that God would move on a prophet spontaneously, there were just as many times that He would give them prophecy in advance and then tell them to deliver it at a later time. Prophetic dance, then, is not synonymous with spontaneous dance. Spontaneous dance can be prophetic, but the two are not necessarily one and the same. This distinction is important for a couple of reasons. First of all, the prophet's job is to discern the mind, season, and workings of God and to speak His words on His behalf at His leading. The claim to be dancing prophetically should bear the same nature. We are not dancing prophetically because we just got up and started dancing. If we are truly dancing prophetically, it is because there is something that God has given us to communicate through dance, whether it is spontaneous or not.

Secondly, if we go forth claiming to be speaking on God's behalf and He does not manifest Himself because of our ignorance or presumption, people will not think that *we* are not who we say we are, they will think that *God* is not who He says *He* is.

Nomenclature is important. Aside from those who distinguish themselves as a prophet who dances, everyone who sets themselves to hear God about their dance and then does what they've heard is engaging in prophetic dance every time they dance according to what they've heard.

The Effect of Dance.

Mk. 6:22-26 (AMP)

For when the daughter of Herodias herself came in and danced, she pleased and fascinated Herod and his guests; and the king said to the girl, Ask me for whatever you desire, and I will give it to you. And he put himself under oath to her, Whatever you ask me, I will give it to you, even to the half of my kingdom. Then she left the room and said to her mother, What shall I ask for [myself]? And she replied, The head of John the Baptist! And she rushed back instantly to the king and requested, saying, I wish you to give me right now the head of John the Baptist on a platter. And the king was deeply pained and grieved and exceedingly sorry, but because of his oaths and his guests, he did not want to slight her [by breaking faith with her].

This passage has long been used by opponents to justify why the dance does not belong in the church: John the Baptist was beheaded because the dancer seduced the king. Besides the fact that I vehemently disagree with that line of thinking, I believe that it does more to show the impact of the dance on those who observe it.

Some time ago, the Spirit of God brought me to this passage and He told me to take away the moral assignment. Take away the fact that the daughter's dance resulted in John's death and simply look at the impact the dance had on the king. The king was so moved by the daughter's dancing that he vowed to give her whatever she wanted, up to half his kingdom. She must have been working it out! Now, let's think about what that means.

A kingdom is an area ruled by a king. You and I, though ultimately accountable to the supreme King, have been given temporal rulership over our vessel, which would make our self our kingdom. God does not physically force us to obey Him or to come into relationship with Him. We will ultimately account for our choices but for right now, we have the power to choose how we will and will not participate.

The dance impacted the king so much that he was willing to surrender control of up to half his kingdom. If Herodias' daughter were to take all 50%, he would no longer be able to make any kingdom decisions without her consultation. Our relationship with God is much what their relationship would be if Herodias' daughter took all 50%: a 50/50 partnership. Just as we can't do anything in God's purpose without Him and what He brings to the partnership, He can't do anything in the earth without us and what we bring to the partnership. I do not know the psychological and spiritual specifics of why dance is so impactful to those watching it, but it has the ability to get its viewer to let their gates down and to provoke in them an openness to surrender and cooperation. When I was in the Hush Company, Stacy and LaQuin would always tell me that our job was just to open the hearts of the people long enough to allow the Holy Spirit to get in and begin His work.

On the Matter of Choreography

What have we discussed thus far about our purpose for being before God's people in dance?

- We facilitate the interaction between God and His people and between God's word and His people.
- We reinforce truth that has been dispensed to the people through reiterating the message in our songs.

Sometimes, though, our function is more nuanced. Sometimes we go forth to till and break up fallow ground in the heart and in the atmosphere. As I was researching fallow ground, I came across a blog post by Pastor Benny Keck of First Baptist Church Dover. In his teaching about fallow ground, he explained that it "has to do with farming. It is ground that was once cultivated in the past but for some reason the farmer has allowed it to remain unplowed and uncultivated during the present growing season. The ground has now become hardened and will no longer be [receptive or] productive until or unless it is plowed (broken up) again."[32]

We till the heart so that the experiences of the first three Luke 8 hearers don't become the reality of the people sitting in our churches. We till the heart as we lead the people in praise and worship, as we lead them in gratitude toward God, and as we lead them in remembrance of who God is to them and for them, and what He has done in them and for them. We till the heart when we encourage them in worship to release their anxious and worried grasp on their situation, let down their defenses, and receive the Comforter, the Deliverer, the Healer, the Way-Maker, the Miracle-Worker.

We till the atmosphere when we lift up a praise and worship to God, creating a fragrant environment that compels Him to draw near, that welcomes Him to enthrone Himself in the midst of His people who are passionate and full of expectation for Him.

At other times we go forth to plant, sowing a word and image of instruction, information, or admonishment. Still, at other times we go forth to water, to irrigate, to encourage the harvest to continue coming forth and the spirit to keep pressing forward to obtain the promise. Within the reasons God has us before His people, what specifically is the purpose for the choreography?

When the Holy Spirit leads us to a song (whether instrumental or with lyrics) it is because there is something to be communicated, either to God in praise and/or worship, or to the people in declaration or admonition. If that is the case, then the purpose of our choreography is to give what is to be communicated a physical vehicle for expression.

In my head, there is this kind of spectrum of how intricately we are used to convey that expression. As for myself, I know that God uses me on

---

[32] http://firstbaptistdover.org/pastors-first-blog/

the far right of this spectrum. The underpinning of my assignment in dance is to give body to the word through interpretation. To interpret means to "bring out the meaning of, to give or provide the meaning of, to convey or represent the spirit or meaning of [a thing or idea] in performance."

When I am preparing to minister a song, I do intensive study on the structure and words, what they mean, how they're said in attitude and volume, etc. I study the song until I know the exact timing between words and how long a single word is spoken. Every inflection of the voice- I know where it is and I know its pattern. I study a song to the point where I can minister the song like I was the song. That is how God uses me. That is how He taught me to prepare in my assignment. Regardless of where He uses you along this spectrum, we all dance to give physical expression to that unction, that message, that praise in our spirit.

I would like to share some things with you that I've had to settle within myself as I've matured in ministry. I would also like to share with you five principles God has taught me that guide me as a choreographer in ministry.

It is Settled.

I have been ministering through dance for twenty years and in that time I have experienced a range of emotions and perspectives about myself as a dancer, a choreographer, a technician, and a minister. In this season of maturity, I have settled in these truths:

1. That I am a facilitator between God and His people
2. That it is not my responsibility to come up with choreography. My job is to simply position myself to hear and bring forth what I've heard or seen in my spirit
3. That Him being glorified through my obedience means more to me that having the best dance moves
4. That it is okay for me to desire to be technically excellent and He is supportive of that desire
5. That my desire to be excellent and perceived as "good" must not supersede my desire to direct the attention to Him, the reason I do what I do
6. That my excellence is not in the moves I do, but in the way I serve Him

The five principles He has taught me as a minister and choreographer are as follows:

Principle #1: Understand that you are collaborating with the living Word who communicates through more than words. Therefore, when you interpret His word, you are interpreting more than just a literal word.

As we give body to the Word, we have to look at doing so in the context of our function. As vessels, our main function is to give the Word a body to express itself through. Knowing that, we must acknowledge that we are collaborating with the living Word. Like His creation, the Word communicates with more than just audible sounds. He also communicates with attitude, context, and intention.

When something is spoken, the meaning of those words are not just shaped by the actual words spoken, but also the situation surrounding what was said (context), and the way the words were spoken (in terms of volume, attitude, body language, etc.) We know that meaning changes based on these factors. You can say the same exact words in the same exact order; and depending on how you say it, the meaning can shift significantly. When I interpret a song, my quest is to say it in my body in the way that I hear Him saying it in the song and in my spirit.

Principle #2: Take the time to let God illuminate your spirit and coat your movement with the logos of His word so that you can deliver it in all the nuance and richness He intended.

When we are preparing to minister, we ask God to lead us to the song He would have us declare. We ask Him to guide us in the movements to do, to use us as vessels and speak through us to His people. But do we ask Him to share with us what was on His mind when He spoke those words in the song we're ministering. Do we inquire about what He was thinking, what He was feeling, what He was referencing?

Some time ago, God shared a powerful truth with me: that He, the same God I speak to about my dance, is the same God who communicated with the psalmist who transcribed His words and melodies into the song I am dancing to. The psalmist and I are dealing with the same Word and with the same God who spoke those words. That same God inspired the psalmist about how to say the words- how loud or quiet, how fast or slow, how percussive or billowy, with authority or deference.

There is a Greek word, logos, which is translated word. It refers to the written word; but it also speaks to the reasoning, the thoughts, the computations behind the words. Logos is not just what I said, but what I was thinking when I said it, what led me to say it, what I meant in saying it. The words we minister through dance have logos in them. They were said for a reason. They follow a line of thought. They are housed within an intention. If we give Him the time, God, the author, will willingly share with us what is on His mind concerning the words He has spoken. The psalmist communicates the logos of the words in the way they sing the lyrics, in the volume they use, in the instrumentation. As dancers, we communicate the logos of those same words through the energy we use, through the positions our bodies take on, through the part of our body we use.

Principle #3: Make it a priority to pursue the word in season. See yourself as a communication conduit, set yourself to hear what you should say (song), and then say it through your vehicle as He has led (movement).

Bishop McClendon has shared with us that He does not study to preach. He studies to live. He preaches what He hears, according to Mt. 10:27, which says "Whatever I tell you in the dark, speak in the light; and what you hear in the ear, preach on the housetops." Once he hears it, he spends time with God over what he heard to receive further instruction, revelation, clarification, etc. This was such a moment of clarity for me when he said this to us.

It is so important that we see ourselves as those who declare the word of God through a particular vehicle. Many times I have heard dance ministers say things like "I dance to worship God;" which is true. Our dance is a worship unto God and we are giving praise to His name when we dance before Him and about Him. But, if that is all we are doing, we can do that in the comfort of our own homes. God did not call us to stand before His people so that they could watch us in a session of personal worship between ourselves and Him. He drafted us so that we could come into agreement with Him, use our dance to communicate what He leads, and invite Him into the atmosphere and/or situation we are ministering in.

If we see ourselves in dance ministry as communication conduits, as well as praisers and worshippers, we will attend to our responsibility to seek God about the songs we declare and the movements we use.

Principle #4: The desire for better is good. We are to be continually increasing what He gave us. And yet, more knowledge brings greater ability to move without God and greater temptation to do so. Be vigilant to lay all your new knowledge at His feet and resist allowing the knowledge to decrease your dependence on His leading. As you learn more, press in more.

In Jn 12:49, Jesus declares, "For I have not spoken of myself; but the Father which sent me, He gave me a commandment, what I should say, and what I should speak." The word "of" in this verse means "out from within, out of the depths of the source."

Jesus literally spoke the words. They came from out of His mouth. And He was a learned man who was very wise and knew a lot of things. He had thoughts and answers in Himself. So, what did He mean when He said He did not speak of Himself? He made a conscious decision to submit His wisdom, His thoughts, His answers to the leading of the Father. He could have handled things differently. He could have answered situations differently. But, He chose to only answer as the Father directed Him.

As we go on our various journeys to become better dancers, technicians, and choreographers; as we cultivate our gifts and raise the level of excellence in dance ministry, we must be careful not to let our desire to be relevant supersede our choice to submit our knowledge and abilities to His direction, though we may be capable of so much more than what He leads us to do. We must settle in ourselves that obeying Him, being a facilitator for Him and His people, Him being glorified means more to us than having dance moves that draw comments on Facebook, get us booked at other churches and conferences, or win us an "America's Most" award.

Principle #5: As we dance according to the direction of the Spirit of God, He is using our obedience to speak.

As we dance, God is ministering to the people about what He is saying in what they see us doing and how it applies to them. As He spoke through Ezekiel's demonstrations, He will do the same though ours if we position ourselves to hear and then bring forth what we've heard.

Form and Training.

In the first edition of this book, this section looked at forms of dance used in ministry, particularly questioning whether there were any forms of dance that should not be used in ministry. When I was first writing this book, the great influx of trained professional dancers into ministry was in its infancy. This influx brought with it a rift in the dance ministry community over what movements were suitable for ministry and whether trained dancers and their secular movement had a place in God's dance. I pray that we have matured out of this sidedness because it is silly. Paul calls it carnal in 1 Cor. 3:4 (NKJV). He asks his audience "For where *there are* envy, strife, and divisions among you, are you not carnal and behaving like *mere* men?" Paul's audience was dividing themselves based on who raised them in the faith, what they've been taught and all the doctrinal issues and practices that come with that. They were all of the same faith, but petty in their measuring one assignment and grace in the kingdom against another.

We commit this same act of immaturity when we attempt to measure each other's fitness for service based on how we got here or the differences in the way God has given us to execute our assignment.

Ps. 24:1 tells us "The earth is the Lord's, and all its fullness, The world and those who dwell therein." Col. 1:16 tells us "For by him were all things created, that are in heaven, and that are in earth, visible and invisible, whether *they be* thrones, or dominions, or principalities, or powers: all things were created by him, and for him." *All things* includes us, our bodies, and all the potential ways our bodies can move. If this is true, what designates a movement as appropriate or inappropriate to worship God with? Who makes that determination? Further, why are we so often trying to make the determination of appropriateness for someone else's assignment?

The Lord led me to Acts 10 as a lens through which we could understand this issue. Acts 10 is basically the account of Cornelius, a centurion who was not Jewish but loved God and was active in his faith. An angel of the Lord came to Cornelius to tell him his prayers had been heard and to go find Simon Peter and hear him. This trips up Simon Peter, who is a Jewish man, because according to Jewish law, "a Jewish man was not to keep company with or go to one of another nation (v. 28)." But God instructs Simon Peter not to call common or unclean what He (God) has cleansed (v.15). Later Peter tells Cornelius when they finally meet that God essentially told him: better yet, don't call *any man* common or unclean (v.28)

As Simon Peter is ministering to them, he shares God's revelation to him about grace: "In truth I perceive that God shows no partiality. But in every nation whoever fears Him and works righteousness is accepted by Him (v. 34-35)." And we go on to see these men, deemed unclean and not fit to even be in the same company as a Jew, receive the Holy Spirit and be baptized. By grace, they received what started with the Jew, but was always purposed to be available to anyone who wanted it.

Through the lens of this account let's look at dance and the issue of fitness, or the lack thereof, to be used by God. Before we do, I want to highlight a couple of important parts of the account in Acts 10:

1. God approached Cornelius, the "unclean" man
2. God led the "unclean" man to Simon Peter knowing the Jewish law
3. God called Cornelius, the non-Jew, clean and chose to fill him with the His Holy Spirit knowing he was not a Jew

As it pertains to the dance, the same principle that applies to man, that anyone who fears Him and works righteousness is accepted, applies to the dance. How do we fear God and work righteousness in our dance? The word fear is the Greek word *phobeo*, and it means "to reverence, venerate, to treat with deference or reverential obedience." We know through verses like Eccl. 12:13 and Deut 6:2 that fearing the Lord is keeping His commandments to us; it is basically proceeding according to His leading. So we fear the Lord in our dance when we seek Him about how we should go forth in ministry (what song we dance to, what moves we do, what we wear, etc) and go forth in dance according to what He has showed us. Righteousness pertains to God's way of being and acting right.[33] We work righteousness in our dance, again, when we seek the Lord about how He would have us to go forth, when we lay our ambitions in dance, our opinions about dance, our insecurities about dance, our hang-ups about dance, and our presumptions about dance at His feet and truly allow Him to lead our dance in the way it should go.

---

[33] Bishop McClendon

So are there any movements that are unclean and should not be offered in worship to God? Honestly, that should not be the focus of our inquiry. Dancers, God drafted you to serve Him in dance knowing what kind of dancer you are. I encourage you not to take on the burden and anxiety of trying to police your movement to make sure it is not offensive to others. Your only job is to make sure you position yourself to hear God about your dance and proceed according to what He has led you to do. That's it. Like God said to Jeremiah, "Do not be afraid of their faces, For I *am* with you to deliver you. (Jer. 1:8)"

When God shows up in response to your worship because you obeyed Him, what else is there to say? What else is there to dispute? If God accepts your dance and blesses it, who cares if anyone has a problem with the fact that your hip moved too much for their comfort or their tradition? Serve God with your whole heart and your whole body and dust the rest of that madness off your feet and keep moving.

Dance ministry community, we need to allow grace and love to engulf and fill us. We need to let grace influence how we treat one another, how we talk about each other, how we view one another, how we cover one another. We need to allow room for the diversity of God to flourish in each other's dance and not be so quick to make determinations about dance that doesn't look like ours, dance that doesn't happen in the same contexts our does, or dancers that don't wear the same garments we do. God gave us the room to grow into what He gave us. We need to extend the same room for growth to others. It is right to hold each other accountable but it must be done in a spirit of love and concern for part of *our* body, as we are all part of the same body. And, it is to be done for the purpose of edifying the hearer. It hurts my heart when I read snarky, condescending comments on social media about issues such as dancers and their garments. We can't do that to family. God didn't do that to us when we were young in ministry and didn't know any better. What gives us the right to do that to another child of His, and more so, a part of us? Let God be God and let us focus on working righteousness in our own assignment.

On the Issue of Training

On the issue of training, this is another unnecessary area of contention. As we all have a different assignment, we all have different paths and different ways we have come into dance ministry. God knows that and we need to be okay with that. Both the technically trained dancer and the dancer with little or no training have their own crosses to bear. God uses skilled artisans but He also uses a willing heart regardless of the level of skill and will confound the presumption of those who think their skill makes them more qualified for use than others. We know this. But I want to encourage both to continue to press forward in the excellence of your service to God, whatever that looks like for what He has given you to do.

To the untrained dancer I want to first say thank you for your willingness to step out into strange territory to be an available vessel. I had no training when I started. You paved the way and tilled the ground for the many dancers who have come behind you. Your heart and your willingness to obey is what God is after. At the same time, though God called you and utilized you in an untrained state, He did not necessarily intend for you to *stay* untrained. For those who believe this to be so, let me tell you that your lack of training does not make you a more usable vessel. Just as God expects us to grow in all other aspects of our life, He expects us to apply ourselves to strengthening and perfecting His gifts within us. This means different things for different people. For some, it may mean joining a dance class. For others it may not. It may mean declaring a dance major in college, or simply buying dance videos, or spending time in the presence of God and letting Him teach you movement that He has for you. Whatever it is, it is right to invest in expanding your gift.

To the trained dancer, let me say thank you for investing the fruits of all your years of training into the Kingdom. You are just as valuable and critical to the Kingdom of God. God absolutely uses skilled workmen. For you, the issue is submitting your training to the leading of the Holy Spirit. This does not mean that you have to abandon all that you have worked to accomplish. It simply means that five pirouettes, although *very* impressive, have no place in your ministry unless God directed you to do them. Just as the lack of training does not make one more qualified for ministry, neither does the abundance of training. God will use *whoever* is willing to receive His leading, and He will show up for whoever sets themselves to obey.

As a dancer in and outside the church, I understand your struggle. For years, you have spent massive amounts of time training your body to become dependent on your technique as it keeps you from injury and helps you move with ease. It also helps you identify your movement preferences, which influences your choices in choreography. When you function in ministry, though, there has to be a mental shift from relying solely on your technique, to submitting your tendencies to God and relying on the technique for movement only. You have to lay it at His feet and say Lord, I place this all at your disposal and I will only use it to serve Your purpose in the way that You lead.

Worshipping God in "Non-Church" Contexts

This was interesting when the Lord put this on my heart to include in this second edition. I did not talk about this when I first wrote the book because, frankly, I knew nothing about it back then. But my life has changed dramatically since I first wrote this book, as has the reality of dancers in the Kingdom. So, what about those of us whose assignments exist "outside the church?"

First I want to acknowledge that there is a large range of how we are used outside of the church building. Some of us dance in secular contexts but have overtly Christian messages in our dance. We dance in a group of Christian dancers to Christian songs, etc. Others of us operate more covertly. We may be a group of Christian dancers and our dances have Kingdom underpinnings but are not so overtly doctrinal; or we may be the only Christian in a group of dancers, not dancing about anything remotely having to do with our God or our faith (assuming we have sought the Lord about it). What about us?

The foundational thing we must realize is that we are the church. It goes where we go so we are never outside the church. Further, there is biblical endorsement for us who operate outside of the building. In Mt. 13, Jesus tells us that the field is the world and that He has sown His children into that world. We are to be like Him, who, in Jn. 17, tells us that He was in the world, but not of it. We, therefore, do not lose one iota of our anointing or access to the power of God available to us just because we aren't inside of a building with a pulpit.

As for how ministry happens in our assignment, it happens for us the same way it happens for our brethren inside the building – we must be led by the Spirit of God and move according to His leading. But, you might ask, how am I ministering if I am not openly talking and dancing about God and my faith? You minister by being the fragrance of Christ and His love to those around you (2 Cor. 2:5). You emit that fragrance in the way you treat people, in your integrity, in your work ethic, in your peace of mind and groundedness, in your excellence at what you do. You minister by being salt and light to those around you (Mt. 5:13). Salt is a preserver and God will deal with those in your environment based on His covenant with you, like in Sodom and Gomorrah where He was willing to consider sparing the region because of His relationship with Abraham. In Josh. 1:3 and Deut 11:24, God promises that everywhere we put our foot is given to us. Given to us to do what? To expand His Kingdom where we are and to be His body there.

God may lead you to pray for people and they might never know you did it. They may never find out or realize that you are a Christian at all. God might give you influence with co-workers and lead you in what to minister to them even if you don't not include all the Christian language you would use in an openly Christian conversation. He will give you Kingdom language. You minister by dancing, even if it is not to Christian music or anything related to Christianity. You are the one who determines your life and your dance to be a worship to God. You hold the ability to invite Him to be glorified in what you do. You might be in a dance about non-Christian subject matter for an audience of non-Christians, but God reaches out to someone through your worship and they are drawn to you and don't understand why, giving you an open door to speak into their life. These are just some of the ways ministry happens through you. Just be who you are. You don't have to announce it or beat people over the head with it for it to be true. I don't start every sentence and interaction with "as a black woman..." I am a black woman whether I tell everyone or not. Besides, your fruit will speak louder than anything you could possibly say.

> *You are the one who determines your life and your dance to be a worship to God. You hold the ability to invite Him to be glorified in what you do.*

When the Minister Needs Ministry

In ministry, we are always pouring out, seeking God in order to attend to the needs of others. But, what happens when we are the ones who need ministry? What are we to do when attacks of discouragement or disorder hit our lives but we still have ministry obligations? What happens when our home life or finances are acting wacky but we still have rehearsal? What happens when we feel completely disconnected from the reason we do what we do and our love for God doesn't seem to be enough to keep us content and satisfied in our service to Him? What do we do when our personal life is fine but our attitude about serving God has shifted? What happens when all the rehearsals, the repetition, the sore bodies, the fasting, missing another family get together, having to turn down another concert you really want to see just no longer seems worth it? What about when we have given access to confusion, apathy, and discord into our ministries, and we no longer want to come to rehearsal because we don't want to deal with each other? Or, how about when we find ourselves dragging our minds and bodies into rehearsal while wishing we were anywhere else but here? What do we do as leaders when we begin to question our own reasons for serving, when we feel like we have lost our way, when we feel like we don't know which way the ministry is supposed to go anymore; when it feels like we have lost the clarity of purpose and direction we once had, but we still have to show up and lead rehearsal because everyone is looking at us for instruction?

Our ministry has experienced this kind of dry spell, really it was a season of drought. It was a crippling feeling for me as a leader as I felt like I was wasting my member's time, losing their attention and respect, and disappointing my Father because I didn't know what to do. I felt like I was failing. I couldn't sense the right direction personally or as a leader. Somehow our ministry as a whole became disconnected from the reason we got into this in the first place. We still loved God just as much as before, but we lost sight of where our actions and our service fit in that love. Showing up to rehearsal week after week with nothing to give made me painfully aware that I had reduced what I did to dance moves, without even realizing it. No matter what choreography we came up with, it was empty. And I felt it. I felt the disconnection and it was painful. I wanted the "more" that I once moved in and I began to cry out to the Lord. The cry of my spirit was Lord, fill us again with reverence for what we do. Help us see our activity as more than having to drag ourselves away from home to come learn some dance steps, when we'd much rather be doing something else; as more than having to give up three hours of our life every Friday. Nothing seemed to change for a couple of weeks but we kept showing up, even though we were all struggling not to quit the dance ministry. Then, during one rehearsal, He led me to have each of us answer four questions:

1. Why are you here?
2. What do you personally want to gain from being here? What are you after?
3. What do you want to see happen in this ministry and through this ministry?
4. What do you bring to this ministry? (As it is important for us to see ourselves as contributors, not just passive members)

Afterwards, we all read our answers aloud to each other and then He had us pray. Then our refreshing came. He was faithful to fill us again with perspective and context and He never condemned us for struggling in the grind of our assignment. He ministered to our hearts and dealt with the true issues in them, and they were different for each of us. What I learned that night was that it is okay and normal to go through seasons of drought (whether it be a drought of direction, of passion, of creativity, of will, etc) as long as you know what to do to get back to the water in the well. He ministered several things to us:

- The fulfillment of this call has nothing to do with feeling (whether you feel the passion to do it, feel anointed, feel God, feel like doing it, etc). Keep showing up and receive the grace of God which supplies what you need to keep moving forward.

- Take time to remember why you do this. Be sensitive to when you have reduced this assignment to tasks and begun to function on auto-pilot. Showing up to rehearsal, praying real quick and cranking out dances is the fast route to disconnection.

- Reconnect to the bigger picture, which goes beyond just loving God. How many couples do we know that said they loved each other but still ended up divorcing. You can love each other and still not be in agreement about why the two of you are together, what you're after, where you're headed, or why the struggles still continue to be worth working through. Loving God, alone, is not enough to keep us strong in this working relationship with Him. We have to come together regularly and refresh ourselves in the agreement between the two of us about why we are together and why we should continue together in the way we are going. We have to do regular agreement maintenance, regular vision maintenance, and regular love maintenance.

- Remember that your activity is worship to Him and He has a response to it. Put Him in remembrance of how He said He would respond to you when you worship Him. Remember that your time is just as much a seed as the money you put in an envelope. It is a seed that also releases the law and benefits of seedtime and harvest. He has a response to the seed we sow. Remind Him of what He said He would do when we sow seed and expect Him to do what He said.

- Relieve yourself from the pressure of having to make a dance. Remember the burden is not on us to create or make up. This assignment already has marching orders. It already has assembly instructions. Our burden is to keep ourselves out of the way and in a place where we are consistently freed up to hear and receive.

- See yourself again as a contributor to something you said yes to, not as a prisoner without a choice.

- Realize and never forget how invested our God is in making sure there is not a thing that exists that can hinder us from being available and productive in bringing forth His purposes in the earth. Remember, we have been drafted into His endeavors because He cannot complete them here without a partner-in-flesh. We are in this working relationship with Him as He is building, establishing, and restoring, and we are a necessary part of bringing that to fruition.

But, what happens when we stop building because we put our hammer down so that we can find the rest of the money to pay our house note? What happens to God's kingdom when the foundation ceases to be laid because we put down the concrete so that we could figure out how to solve or address some life issue?

Studies have been done on Google, Inc. and how they have addressed these kinds of concerns in order to get maximum output from their employees. There is a theory called Maslow's Hierarchy of Needs[34] which basically states that an individual cannot reach their full potential in life or in an endeavor until they know that their basic needs (food, shelter, etc) are met and they feel safe and secure in their life and livelihood (in areas like their health, family, and employment, etc). Acknowledging this, Google has devised a work environment that alleviates as many basic need and daily life concerns as possible. This frees their employees to devote the bulk of their focus to investigating, creating, and refining Google products. To this end, their headquarters house first-class dining facilities, gyms, laundry rooms, child care, pet care, massage rooms, carwashes, dry cleaning, commuting buses, on-site oil change service, car wash, dry cleaning, massage therapy, hair stylists, fitness classes and bike repair services, just to name a few. Basically, they have made it so that their employees don't have to worry about how any of their living concerns will be taken care of. They don't even need to leave the premises because the services are at their job; therefore their productivity can be maximized.

In Mt. 7:11, the writer poses this question: if we know how to give good things to our children, how much more does our God have the desire, capacity, willingness, and intention to give us good things? If Google, Inc., who is not God, can so take care of their employees, leaving them unburdened and free to produce, how much more has our God, the maker of all things, created such an environment for us to thrive in? 2 Ptr. 1:3-4 tells us that God "has given to us all things that *pertain* to life

---

[34] A theory in psychology proposed by Abraham Maslow

and godliness…" Ps. 37:5 instructs us to "commit [our] way unto the LORD; trust also in him; and he shall bring *it* to pass." Pr. 16:3 tells us to "commit [our] works unto the LORD, and [our] thoughts shall be established." By these three verses, we can be assured that there is nothing pertaining to our living or our godliness that His word and power have not addressed and taken care of; therefore we, too, are free to live unburdened and fruitful. In Mt. 16:25 and Lk. 9:24, Jesus tells us that if we put our life and its concerns entirely out of our way[35] for the sake of His concerns, we shall meet up with[36] our life again with our concerns having been handled. Mt 6:33 reiterates this, telling us to seek first the kingdom of God and all the other things (whatever those are for us) will be added to us.

We have to be settled in the security He has given us: that as we put the concerns of our life out of our way and give them to Him, He is faithful to take care of our needs while we are tending to His business. Therefore, I don't have to cancel rehearsal because I'm trying to find a way to make my house payment. Instead, I give it to Him in prayer and I go take care of His business. I go to rehearsal and continue preparing the dance He gave Me, which is going to minister deliverance to someone who Has been seeking Him. My refusal to let my finances stop me from being available shows Him that I trust Him more than I trust any other possible solution. He promised that if I would give my concerns to Him, He would lead me and favor me in dealing with them. So, He responds to my act of trust and faith by giving me instruction on what to do about the money I need and He gives me favor with the bank. My house is secure and His child is able to experience His faithfulness to respond and deliver.

As I was writing this section, God gave me the essence of this point by saying the following:

The assignment I gave you to bring forth in the earth is something that I cannot do. I cannot do in the earth what I have given you to do, which is why I have given it to you. However, I

---

[35] Greek translation for "lose:" *apollymi* – Strong's 622
[36] Greek translation for "find:" *heurisko* – Strong's 622

can take care of your life. I can heal your body. I can give you favor with managers and CEOs. I can orchestrate divine appointments with people you need to meet and work with. I can cause someone to give you the money you need. I can give you the strategy to take your product international. I can cause the banker to approve your business loan. I can move the creditor to forgive your debt. I can bring healing to your family and your marriage. I can protect your children. I can do that. But I cannot do what I have given you to do. I cannot do anything in this realm without a body. You are My body, and when you turn your attention away from My purpose to tend your life issues, you leave Me and My purpose homeless and hostage in a place where I can do nothing about it but wait for someone else who will take Me at My word and let Me use them to get My work accomplished here. You don't need to tend the issues of your life. I've got your life issues, so we both don't need to be handling them. You cannot do with your life issues what I can do. And I cannot do in this earth what you can do. That is why I tell you not to worry about your life. I have your life. I have always had your life. And now I need you to trust Me with it, as I have trusted you with Mine.

RECAP

- It is not our job to come up with choreography. Our job is to position ourselves to hear and then dance according to what we've heard.

- When we put the word of God into song, it helps us stay consciously connected to the word and it helps ensure the remembrance of that word.

- We must be attentive to what is being declared over the pulpit because it is our job to reinforce the offices' efforts to help the people stay connected to the word long enough for it to produce fruit in their lives.

- Physical demonstration, which includes dance, is a part of the way God speaks.

REFLECTION QUESTIONS

➢ How has this chapter informed, clarified, and/or adjusted my understanding and perception of the importance and impact of the songs I minister and the movements I dance?

➢ With greater understanding, what do I need to shift and adjust in the way I approach choreography and song selection?

➢ How diligently am I connecting the songs I minister to what is being preached in my church? What do I need to adjust in this area?

➢ How diligent am I in seeking God about what song and movements to do?

➢ What does this new understanding bring to how I minister through dance?

➢ What am I speaking about my ministry? My movements? My song choices? The other dancers in my ministry? My ministry's relationship with the house and the other departments within the house? God's response to my dance? The people that receive my ministry?

➢ What scriptures am I standing on concerning the above areas?

➢ Based on what was covered in this chapter, write a prayer to God about the songs and choreography used in your ministry. Include what you desire to accomplish through Him and Him through you.

4

Entering Ministry

As we have taken this journey, I hope that you can clearly see that dance ministry is more than an activity at the church. It is more than a 5th Sunday time filler. It is a viable vehicle that God *is* using in ministry to His people and in the establishing of His kingdom in the earth. I felt led to make this case, showing the responsibility and impact of the dance minister, before talking about answering the call to this vehicle of ministry.

I used to get a lot of questions about starting in dance ministry. In asking, what dancers usually wanted to know were the practical things like the classes they should take, whose workshop they should attend, or how they should go about recruiting dancers. These are all important questions to ask. However, when starting in ministry, there is a more foundational issue that must be attended to, which will lead to the answers we are seeking.

In the first chapter, we established that the dance is not the ministry and the ministry is not the dance. Dance is the vehicle that we use to fulfill our ministry. Our ministry is to hear God concerning our dance and proceed accordingly. Before we can proceed to anything, though, we first have to know what He has for us to do. How do we get this instruction that we will use our dance to fulfill? As we prepare to answer this, let us first look at three principles:

1. God brings us into a readied work that is set for its finish.

Everything our ministry will actualize into is already created and planned out, leaving us to simply show up and proceed as directed. Despite knowing this we deal in ministry as if it were something needing to be created, made from scratch, and more, as if we are the ones that need to do the creating. But, God actually brings us into a readied work that is set for its finish. What do I mean by this?

In clothing and furniture manufacturing there is a term called finishing which is an entire process unto itself. In these terms, the finish is the work required for the completion of the final touches. A finisher takes a particular product in its conceptualized, but unassembled form through a process that produces what we eventually see at the store or in a catalog. Their job includes the finishing steps of shaping, assembling, adjusting, smoothing, painting, polishing, cleaning, and decorating[37] the item they are working on. By the time the product gets to them, the color paint they will use has already been determined, as well as the shape it will be, what pieces will be assembled together, the decorations that will be carved into it, what it will be used for, etc.

Likewise, the work God calls us to is already conceptually developed, but unassembled in the earth. It already has an identity, specific aim and purpose. It already comes with a course of action. By the time we get involved, what that work is and is to look like has already been determined and planned. Its various parts are ready and waiting. It doesn't need to be created or thought out, just assembled and finished.

2. Just so shall you make it.

Ministry is service. It is action done at the direction of another, and more, action that corresponds to the instruction given by another. If that is so, there must *first* be instruction to act upon. As the finisher simply produces the already determined specifications for a product, so we are to find out and produce the already determined specifications for the work God has assigned to us.

---

[37] Webster's Unabridged Dictionary

3.   Our general call to dance is different from what we are individually assigned to do with the dance.

Ps. 119:105 (KJV) says God's word is a "lamp unto our feet and a light unto our path." Bishop McClendon explained that a lamp is a general wash of light, which usually illuminates everything in a room. This is the general direction we as the Body of Christ are all commonly going in, and more specifically the general call to dance that all dance ministers share. A light, he explained, is a more focused, sharper source. A flashlight does not light an entire room but instead only lights the specific object it is focused on. Within the macrocosm of dance ministry, it is important for each of us to seek out where God is pointing the flashlight for our particular course and assignment.

If I am hosting a party, everyone coming to my party shares a common purpose: getting there. However, within that common purpose of getting to my party, each has a specific, different path and method. Some will take the bus, some the car, others will fly. Some will use the 101 freeway and others will use the 5 freeway. Others will take side streets. Some will come in SUV's and others in compact or luxury cars. These specific paths and methods of achieving the common purpose are like the diversity and specificity of our individual paths within our common purpose in the dance. Your ministry to God is the rendering of your obedience to what He showed you, specifically and individually, and that will look different than my ministry to Him.

With these three principles in mind, let us now examine this process by which God establishes us in ministry.

Step #1: Perceiving and Understanding the Call.

Though we can generally sense when the call of God has come to us, like ministry, our understanding of what it really is sometimes gets drowned in spiritual ambiguity. This has presented a problem, as ambiguity has left us uncertain about how to properly respond once we sense calling. 97% of the questions I receive from dance ministers, of all positions, are a result of having too general of an understanding of its nature and purpose. Well, what is calling? And what is God's intention concerning it?

What is the call of God?

Although there are supernatural aspects to it, calling, or the call of God to you and I is still a very practical and discernable interaction. Some time ago, the Lord began to answer some questions I had about calling and the process of entering into public ministry. Most of us have heard the phrase "many are called, but few chosen." I too had heard this but I didn't understand the difference between them. I tried to understand it by looking up the Strong's definitions, but I still was unclear until Bishop McClendon clarified it for me one day while preaching. He said the chosen were the called that waited to be sent. About a year later, the Spirit of God led me to Mt. 22:1-14 (NKJV) and began to explain to me what that meant:

> And Jesus answered and spoke to them again by parables and said:
> *2* "The kingdom of heaven is like a certain king who arranged a marriage for his son, *3* and sent out his servants to call those who were invited to the wedding; and they were not willing to come.
> *4* Again, he sent out other servants, saying, 'Tell those who are invited, "See, I have prepared my dinner; my oxen and fatted cattle are killed, and all things are ready. Come to the wedding." ' *5* But they made light of it and went their ways, one to his own farm, another to his business. *6* And the rest seized his servants, treated them spitefully, and killed them. *7* But when the king heard about it, he was furious. And he sent out his armies, destroyed those murderers, and burned up their city. *8* Then he said to his servants, 'The wedding is ready, but those who were invited were not worthy. *9* Therefore go into the highways, and as many as you find, invite to the wedding.' *10* So those servants went out into the highways and gathered together all whom they found, both bad and good. And the wedding hall was filled with guests. *11* But when the king came in to see the guests, he saw a man there who did not have on a wedding garment. *12* So he said to him, 'Friend, how did you come in here without a wedding garment?' And he was speechless. *13* Then the king said to the servants, 'Bind him hand and foot, take him away, and cast him into outer darkness; there will be weeping and gnashing of teeth.' *14* For many are called, but few are chosen."

This parable is mainly about response to the Jews for their refusal to accept Jesus Christ as the prophesied Savior and Messiah. But within that, it is also a very revealing illustration of the process of calling, the response to it, and the consequences of not going through this process correctly. The setting for this parable is a wedding feast which the king is throwing for his newly married son. Various people throughout the community have been invited to the wedding feast. The king instructs his servants to bring the invitees to the feast but they reject his invitation. He then instructs his servants to go out again and bring back anyone who is willing to come. The servants go out and bring people back to the feast, both desirable and undesirable, but all willing. The king comes in to welcome his guests and, out of all his other guests, he notices a single man who is not wearing a wedding garment. He confronts the man about his inappropriate attire and the confrontation ends with the man being thrown out of the party and into outer darkness. Jesus then concludes the parable with this statement: "For many are called, but few chosen." What does that statement mean and what does it have to do with calling?

I began to study the words "called" and "chosen" and I found some interesting things. The word "called" is an adjective and it describes those who have been invited.[38] An invitation is a request [for one] to participate, be present or take part in something.[39] The call of God, that pulling we feel toward a particular area, is God extending an invitation to us. It is Him simply notifying us that He wants us to be a part and a participant in something with Him. His initial request for our participation is not a request for us to *do* anything but show up. At that point, all He is seeking is a conversation. This can be better understood if we apply it to receiving an invitation to a party.

When we receive an invitation to an event, the information it provides is only general information, like the date, time, place, and address of the event, the occasion, and sometimes the attire and parking instructions. That small piece of paper is only designed to alert us that our presence has been requested, to tell us generally what for, and where to go to participate. It does not provide any more information for us to do anything with, except confirm or deny our participation, and show up at the event. The real

---

[38] Strong's #*2822*
[39] Webster's Unabridged Dictionary

interaction happens when we get to the party. Likewise, the call of God is Him asking us to simply show up for a private party of two. It is Him alerting us that our presence and participation has been requested, telling us generally what for, and where to meet Him.

Much like receiving a party invitation, calling comes with some degree of information. Though we understand that the only thing we are to do with the information given on a paper invitation is to simply show up where we have been invited, we somehow fail to apply that understanding to calling. Consequently, with the general and limited sense we have about why God wants to meet with us, we run out and try to do something. Perhaps this is because we have not understood that all calling meant was that God simply wanted to meet with us. The call of God is a call to conversation, not a call to activity. Therefore, we must recognize that there are still other preparative steps before we actually do anything.

I remember Bishop McClendon teaching about calling. He said "when God calls out to you, He wants you to do the same thing your mother wanted you to do when she called you." That one sentence clarified so much for me. What did our mothers want us to do when they called us? For us to run out and go do something? No. They simply wanted us to come and see what they wanted. The same is true for God. Imagine my mother said to me "Lita, come here. I need you to go to the store." How silly would it be for me to jump in the car and drive to the store before I even found out what she wanted from the store, or even what store she wanted me to go to? And yet, many of us find ourselves in this place. God informs us that He wants us to go to the store so we jump in the car and drive to the store, not really sure if we're even at the right store, or what we are there to get. Again, the part about the call of God we misinterpret is that it comes with some sense of why He's calling us. If we don't fully understand the intention of His calling, we think that generally knowing why He called us is all the information we need to go and fulfill the reason He called us, even though a reason has not yet been disclosed. It is obvious that it is ridiculous to run to the store before fully understanding what the person who called us wants from there. Hopefully, in applying this same reasoning to ministry, you can see that more than just a general knowing is necessary. But understand, general information is all calling is intended to provide.

In writing this chapter, a thought occurred to me. I began to wonder if some of us sincerely believe that moving forward under only a general knowledge is an act of faith, where as we go, God will guide our steps. There is a huge difference between the calling of God, where He wants us to come, versus Him giving us the explicit directive to go, and telling us that He will give us more instructions as we go. These are two completely different situations. Unless He specifically tells us to go, and that He will guide us as we go, He is expecting us to come to Him for understanding, instruction, strategy, and insight before we go to do anything. Faith is not ignorant. It has a clear picture of what it is seeking to accomplish. There is a huge difference between acting on faith, and acting without any sense of direction. When David was trying to bring the Ark of the Covenant back to Israel, he thought he was moving in faith. But didn't Uzzah die as a result of participating in David's "faith move?" Why? The Bible says it was because they did not consult God about the proper order in which to bring the Ark back. Faith is action put forth in agreement with, and according to what God has said and instructed, not simply blind hope that He will bless whatever we attempt.

At the beginning of this chapter, I mentioned that I often receive questions from dancers who want to know what they should do once they perceive God calling. When I tell them that they should first sit before Him and let Him clarify some things for them, I can feel their dissatisfaction with my answer. What I want them to know is that I completely understand the zeal and impulse of wanting to go out and immediately start serving God. This zeal is wonderful and I am absolutely positive that He loves it. However, zeal without direction, again, is like going to the store and realizing that you don't know what you're supposed to do there. This quickly leads to frustration, disappointment, distress, and a lot of guessing, wasted time and energy.

Step #2: Answering the Call

We've established the nature and purpose of calling as being invited to talk with God about an assignment. (I am oversimplifying here). Jesus said, "Many are called, but few chosen." The word "chosen" means "to proceed out of what has been shown, disclosed, or revealed." Do you remember how

Bishop McClendon related the called to the chosen? He said, "the chosen are the called who've waited to be sent." To "send" means:

- To dispatch (a person) in a specified capacity
- To propel or discharge with an aim
- To throw or direct in a particular direction
- To dispatch to a specified destination...[40]

If you notice, being sent involves aim, specificity, and particularity. When someone is sent, it is to a specific destination or objective. The sent person knows where they're being sent and what they're being sent to do. As we progress from the state of being called, to the state of being chosen, what is shown, disclosed, and revealed to us will have aim, specificity, and particularity.

Continuing with our store scenario, my mother has called me and said, "Lita, come here. I need you to go to the store." What do I do? I simply go to her and I ask her what she needs from the store. She tells me she wants me to buy her some paper. Though I now know she wants paper, I still only have a general sense of what she wants. This is much like the general knowing that God wants us to do something in the dance. A critical question arises here: with what I know so far, do I have enough information to know when I've gotten the right paper? Many of us get messed up here. We may see that "no" is the obvious answer in this scenario but our dealings with dance ministry show that we have believed the answer to be "yes," that God wanting us to dance is all we need to know. Only further clarification will enable me to be sure I get the right paper. What type of paper does she want? There's writing paper, wrapping paper, tissue paper, paper towels, napkins, and tissue. There's lined paper, see-through paper, and colored paper. How big should the paper be? How much should I get? Does she want it from Michael's, Vons, or Wal-Mart? Is she going to pay by cash, check or credit card? Does she have coupons?

The same degree of specificity needed to get something as simple as paper, is also needed to fulfill our specific assignment in the dance. Like paper, there are many things, besides knowing God wants us to dance, that need to be clarified. Does He want you to join another dance ministry, start

---

[40] Webster's Unabridged Dictionary

one, or assume the lead in an existing one? Is it only for your church home or is it community based? Is it outreach focused? Recreation focused? Who is your ministry specifically designed to reach and minister to? Is there a process for joining your ministry? What is it? What does God want from you and your dancers to prepare you to minister through the dance? Is your ministry to be set up like traditional dance ministries, or is it to be a place where you teach dance and God moves through your teaching and the fellowship?

It is a critical misstep when we don't answer the call and we neglect to show up to the private party. To be sent is to be discharged towards a *specific* objective. God tells us "I want you to do something with the dance," and we enthusiastically say, "Okay," and we're out the door. But, even within the dance there are different and specific objectives. Remember, the dance is only the vehicle used to accomplish what He will disclose to us.

Once God calls us, how is it that we come to know what specific destination or objective He has in mind for us? Specificity is only disclosed in the ever-so-vital private meeting, the season of meeting with God that occurs when we answer the call. What actually happens is we go through a season of briefing.

The Season of Briefing.

A briefing is when you are given instructions and preparatory information for a task you are about to undertake.[41] The person briefing you coaches you thoroughly for the task, and imparts up-to-the minute information and explicit instructions for how you are to complete the task.[42]

These seasons are times of massive disclosure which you leave with a clarity and focus that is other-worldly. You emerge from this time of intimacy with a pattern, a how-to manual for producing and managing what God has entrusted to you. It is here that we receive the specific way we are to individually progress down that general path. In Exodus, God told Moses several times to build according to the pattern that was shown to him on the mountain. To further illustrate this, the Spirit of God gave me the example of a sewing pattern.

---

[41] www.dictionary.com
[42] Webster's Unabridged Dictionary

When you buy a sewing pattern, the pattern comes in an envelope that shows a picture of the garment you will be making. It serves as a guide that will help you gauge whether you're progressing on the right track, by comparing whether or not what you're constructing looks like the picture. In briefing, God will first give you a picture of what it is He wants you to do, one that is more specific than just you dancing. God always starts with vision. Prov. 29:18 (NKJV) says "where there is no [vision],[43] the people cast off restraint." Like the picture on the pattern envelope, vision provides an image that helps you focus your efforts and ensure you're progressing within the constraints of what you've been shown. Everything done within your dance ministry is to be restrained to the purpose of producing or manifesting that picture.

When God began to deal with Moses about building the tabernacle, He first gave him a detailed and descriptive vision of the tabernacle, including information about the materials, dimensions, colors, the people to use to help him build it and what they were to work on, what was to be done in the tabernacle, and how it was to be used and handled. And this was just what was written down for us.

This disclosure will help you make the right decisions and it will help you to know whether you are fulfilling the assignment entrusted to you. If you were told to get Bounty paper towels, there is no need in stressing or praying about whether or not you should get writing paper. You already know what the product you are to bring home should look like. But if all you know is to get paper, there is no way to tell whether you've picked the right one, until you bring it home and are told one way or the other.

Some of us come to realize that, in our haste, we have started with no picture, and we find ourselves unsure of whether our activity is on track or not. This, again, is the danger of thinking that the dance is the ministry. When you think that dance is the ministry you also think that in simply dancing, you are doing what was given for you to do. However, dance is simply a tool used to produce the picture, to fulfill the ministry, which is the obedience. Beyond the dance, to what is all the work of dancing being applied? The wonderful thing about God is that He is gracious, merciful, and invested in our success. If you discover that you have embarked on this

---

[43] KJV

journey without your picture, simply repent and go to Him and get it, and keep moving. It's that simple.

On the back of the pattern envelope, there are guidelines to help you determine how many yards of fabric you will need to produce the picture on the front. Towards the bottom it tells you the fabrics that will work best, and at the bottom it tells you all the other materials, besides the fabric that you will need, like twill tape, zippers, buttons, elastic, etc.

Once He gives you the picture, the vision, He will then tell you what you will need, where to go, and how to get what you need to produce that picture, from the materials to the people. In Ex. 25:3-8 (KJV) God tells Moses what he will need to build the tabernacle: gold, silver, brass, blue, purple, scarlet, fine linen, goats hair, ram skins dyed red, badger's skins, shittim wood, oil for the light, spices for anointing oil and sweet incense, onyx stones and stones for the ephod and breastplate. It is important to note that God will reveal the totality of certain things in one sitting, and others He will reveal progressively, and after you've completed the previous step.

When you open up the pattern envelope, there are two different kinds of paper inside. One is a tissue paper that you can see through, with different kinds of lines and shapes. The other is a regular stock kind of paper that has instructions on it. The tissue paper is the pattern. The shapes and lines on it are the various parts of the garment, like the sleeve, the collar, the waistband, etc. The instructions, on the thicker paper, tell you what shapes to cut out and how to assemble them together. For instance, if I wanted to make pants, I may only need to cut out shapes 1, 2, 4, and 5: the two legs, and the front and back of the waistband. These shapes are to be cut out and pinned to the fabric, which is to be cut out in the same shapes. The instructions then walk you step-by-step through how to sew the various shapes of fabric together to construct the picture on the front of the envelope.

These various shapes are like the various aspects of our dance ministry- how to structure rehearsals, how to discern the people who are to serve with us, how to position ourselves to receive choreography and song, what position to assign people to, and how to know when people are ready to actually stand and minister, etc. As we established earlier, all of these details are already fixed and determined. All we have to do is get the pattern, assemble the pieces as instructed, and make sure what we produce is shaped and assembled just like God showed it to us. The time of briefing is so crucial because that is where we get the pattern for the assignment God has given us to steward.

Managing the various pieces of our dance ministries looks different from person to person, and assignment to assignment. Since the briefing is the only place we get the pattern for our specific assignment in dance, it is very important that we guard against substituting the briefing with other avenues we think will give us the information we need. I have seen dance ministries substitute their time of briefing in three ways:

1. Taking on the assignment of another dance ministry.

When we see a ministry that exemplifies excellence, it is natural to want to pattern ourselves after what we see because we want to be excellent as well. It is good to glean wisdom from each other. No one is expecting each of us to reinvent the wheel. However, we are most excellent when we are fulfilling OUR destiny and path to the best of His ability in us. When you see something that you admire in another ministry, take it to the Lord and ask if it is applicable for your ministry and, if it is, how He would have you implement it. Otherwise, pursue what He has for you and understand that, though it looks different or may be on a different scale, it is just as needed in the Kingdom. See 1 Cor. 12:12-25

2. Trying to get their pattern from dance ministry workshops and conferences.

I can remember years ago when there were hardly any conferences for dance ministry to be found. Now, we are inundated with them. Let me first say that I have nothing at all against conferences and workshops, as I host them myself. When used properly they are a very powerful way of receiving support and disseminating needed information. What I do have a major problem with is what they have become in Christian culture. In our running from conference to conference, there is something vital that we have forgotten: conferences are not meant to give you your assignment; and they cannot replace what can only be gained by spending time in the presence of God. Answering the call and attending your briefing session with Him are the only way you get information specific to your assignment. Conferences are only meant to supplementally equip us with tools and information to support us in producing what God has charged us to do.

As an instructor at a workshop, I can teach you how to multiply and divide. But even in knowing how to multiply and divide, if you, the attendee, don't know what math problems the teacher assigned for you to solve, and you don't apply what I taught you about division to solving THOSE math problems, you have not completed your assignment, even though you now know how to divide. The information given at conferences is only designed to help you solve your assigned math problems, to help you flesh out what God showed you that you were supposed to do in dance. But first, you have to have the assignment. Workshops are not the way we are to answer the call or get the assignment. We should go to workshops *after* we have answered the call, or with the understanding that we still need to answer and attend our briefing.

To the conference attendee: God called *you* to talk to *you* about what He has for your life. He did not call the conference instructor to talk to them about what He has for your life. It is your responsibility and opportunity to commune with Him and find out what He wants with you. Looking to conferences for our assignment is like my mother calling me and me going to my sister. My sister did not call me nor can she tell me why my mother called me. My mother is the only person who can tell me why she called me. Don't be like the children of Israel and give away your responsibility and your opportunity to hear straight from the source for yourself. When God wanted to speak with them, they were afraid and instead told Moses to talk to God and tell them what He said when he got back.[44] The information you receive at workshops is good information but it should not be implemented into your ministry until you have sought God on whether that information should be applied in what He assigned you.

To the conference instructor: It is important for us, as conference hosts, to be honest with what we can really provide for those who come to our workshops. It is also important for us to be honest with ourselves about the reach of the information that God has given us. Was the revelation we received only for our ministry or was it meant to be taught as a method and doctrine? In our teaching, we have to be very careful that we are not facilitating God-avoidance. We must continue to direct them to Him. We

44 Ex. 20:18-21

are dangerously leading them astray if we teach in a way that gives the impression that consulting God after our workshop is unnecessary because they received all the information they would need from us. The truth is God did not give you or I, His instructors, everything His people need to know. We only have a small piece.

    3.   Appropriating Jesus' assignment as their own.
In Isai. 61:1, Jesus declares that He was sent and anointed to preach good tidings to the poor, heal the brokenhearted, proclaim liberty to the captives, and the opening of the prison to those who are bound. I have seen many dance ministries with these listed as their assignment, but these are not our assignment. These are the evidence we leave behind that we have been present there in our assignment.

DNA Evidence of Who's Been in the Room

    In Isa 61:1, Jesus articulates His earthly assignment: to preach good tidings to the poor, heal the brokenhearted, proclaim liberty to the captives, and the opening of the prison to those who are bound. Col. 1:18 says that Christ is the head and we, the church, are His body. Mt 6:22-23[45] tells us that the lamp of the body is the eye, that the body is affected by what comes into the vision of the eye and moves towards what comes into the sight of the mind or spirit. The eyes are in the head and, according to Colossians, Christ is the head. Like natural vision happens in the head, spiritual vision resides with the Head and the body operates according to what the head has fixed its eyes on. Isa. 61:1 tells us the earthly outcomes our Head has fixed His eyes on, that we, His body, are being moved toward to assist in accomplishing.

    1 Cor. 12:12 (AMP) says, "For just as the body is a unity and yet has many parts, and all the parts, though many, form [only] one body, so it is with Christ (the Messiah, the Anointed One)." The human body has many, many parts. Each of those parts has a different function, shape, size, and location within the body, but they each belong to the same body. We know they all belong to the same body because they all share the same DNA, even amidst all their differences.

---

[45] Also Luke 11:34-36

Our DNA is unique to each of us.[46] Each part of our body can be identified as belonging to our body because of that unique DNA it contains. When we interact with objects, through touching, brushing against, laying on, etc., we leave that unique DNA that, when found and examined, informs that we have been present there. Fingerprints are also unique to each person and also leave evidence that we have been there, and/or have at some point touched something that is there.

Isa 61:1 is not our assignment. It is Jesus' earthly assignment and His assignment permeates into every part of His body. It functions like our DNA functions in our physical body. When we go forth in our ministry assignment, we go forth as a part of Christ's body. As every part of our physical body contains the same unique DNA that, upon examination, evinces that it belongs to our body, so do the Isa 61:1 outcomes. When we minister in dance and liberty breaks forth, we have just left DNA evidence that Christ has been in the room. When we minister and healing takes place, we have just left DNA evidence that Christ has been in the room.

Each of us have different ways that we are supposed to leave that DNA evidence in our environments, but the DNA evidence that we leave is the same, despite our differences, because we all belong to the same body. Isa. 61:1 lists DNA markers that are left as evidence that we, Christ's body, have been present in our assignment, and that Christ, therefore, has been in the building.

Knowing this, we can see how important it is that we not take on Christ's assignment as our own. We are involved in His assignment because we are His body. My body is designed to stay alive, healthy, and productive. My heart, liver, and spleen all share in my body's assignment. They all work to help my body stay alive, healthy, and productive. However, each of them has different tasks within my body that contribute to the assignment given to my body. The heart does its thing. The liver does its thing. The spleen does its thing. But all their individual workings are done in order to keep my body alive, healthy, and productive. Like the heart, liver, and spleen each have their own assignment within the body, even though they are all working toward

---

[46] Unless you are an identical twin.

the same purpose as the body, so do we. Thus we have a responsibility to answer the call and find out our part because, as Eph 4:16 tells us, the growth and health of the body and its assignment depend on us doing so.

RECAP

- God brings us into a work that is already created and conceptually developed, but unassembled in the earth. It already has an identity, specific aim and purpose. It already comes with a course of action. It doesn't need to be created or thought out, just assembled and finished.

- Our general call to dance is different from what we are individually assigned to do with the dance. We must seek out the particular course and assignment God has for us individually.

- The call of God is a call to conversation, not a call to activity.

- Answering the call and attending our briefing session with Him are the only way we get information specific to our assignment.

- Isa 61:1 is not our assignment. It is evidence that we, Christ's body, have been present in our assignment, and that Christ, therefore, has been in the building.

REFLECTION QUESTIONS

> What are the specifics of my assignment?

> Who am I called to?

> In what context?

> What should it look like?

> How am I to go about bringing it forth?

> Have I truly given God the opportunity to show me the specific assignment He has for my life and gifts? Have I truly given myself permission to be what God called me to be through dance? Am I modeling my ministry off of someone else's instructions or advice? Am I modeling my ministry off of another's that I admire?

> Based on what was covered in this chapter, write a prayer to God about your assignment through dance. Include what you desire to accomplish through Him and Him through you.

CONCLUSION

When I asked God to help me understand what dance ministry was about, I never in a million years would have thought that six years later I would be writing the closing paragraphs of a book. I really never expected that five years after that I would be finishing a second edition. It is my sincere prayer that this information has answered questions, provided confirmation, and liberated you to obey God according to the uniqueness and specificity that He has crafted you with. I also pray that your spirit has been roused, awakening an insatiable desire to seek God for more information regarding your ministry and the ministry of dance as a whole.

There is a position we must assume that is more fundamental than that of a dancer. In fact, this most fundamental position informs what we do as dancers. If you desire to assume the position of true ministry in dance, then regular communion and consultation with God must be a can't-function-without-it part of your life. The dance is not the ministry and the ministry is not the dance. The position we must assume is not dancer. The position we must assume is of one who continually pursues the presence and voice of God and dances out of what we have seen and heard in His presence.

Dancer, you contribute something very precious and very mighty to the Kingdom of God. The culminating 5-10 minutes you spend dancing reaches far beyond the people in front of you, far out into the destiny of this whole Body. You are valuable. You are needed. And God is ready to work His might and power through you so, Dancer! Assume the Position.

Whatever You Say...

Some time ago the Spirit of God dealt with me regarding what I was speaking over my dancing. It is so important that we declare the word of God over this area. You might be asking what are we supposed to say; there are no direct scriptures for the dancer to speak in faith. We are told to praise God in the dance. We are given instances where dancing was done, but there are virtually no scriptures directly addressing the dancer.

The Spirit of God showed me that even though there are no scriptures specifically to the dancer (besides Psalms 149 and 150), there is an abundance of scripture that can be applied to us in principle. I have listed the scriptures He gave me in the following pages. I encourage you to include them in your prayers, speak them as a daily declaration of faith, and definitely add more to this list.

In his teaching, "Bible Faith," Bishop Mc Clendon taught that faith is always "is." Faith is always present tense because it speaks those things that be not as though they were (right now). The scriptures given, therefore, have been put in the present tense. Make them personal to your situation, your needs and your ministry. Always make sure, however, that you ask the Holy Spirit for guidance so as not to impose on scripture something it was not intended for.

Happy declaring!!

Choreography

Ex. 35:31-35
I am filled with the Spirit of God, in wisdom and understanding, in knowledge and all manner of workmanship to choreograph and design excellent and anointed dances...And I have in my heart the ability to teach.

Ex. 4:12
I go because You are with me teaching me what to say through my dance.

Ex. 25:40
I make it a point to design the dances according to the pattern, which was shown to me in my time with God.

James 1:5
Father, You said if anyone lack wisdom, let him ask for it. I know this is a divine principle so Father I ask you for a fresh infilling of your creativity, that I might design dances as a skilled craftsman. I receive that infilling right now and I thank you for it in Jesus name. Amen.

1 Cor. 2:9-10
The Spirit of God is in me and He reveals to me the deep creativity of God in choreography, lighting ,production and costuming. He shows me dances that eyes have not seen and He gives me music that ears have not heard, nor entered into the hearts of man.

John 12:49-50
I do not speak on my own authority; but the Father who sent me gives me a command what I should say (what song to dance to) and what I should speak (the choreography and visual design). I am led by the Spirit and I do not minister in my own authority, gifting, or agenda. I say exactly what the Father has told me to say, exactly how He said to say it.

Mt. 5:20
The songs You direct me to do and the moves You give me to do, that will I do only. The message You give me in my ear, [through the songs and moves I receive from You], that I will declare through my dance.

Dancers/All
Deut. 12:11
In my dance is where You choose to make Your name (Your nature, character and authority) abide.

Acts 4:29

I speak Your word [through my dance] with all boldness and You stretch out Your hand to heal and signs and wonders are done through the name of Jesus.

Mk. 16:20

As I go out and preach the word through my dance, You work with and confirm the word [I declared through my dance] with accompanying signs and wonders.

Prov 16:3/Ex 25:9/Prov 3:6/Ps 119:105/Mt 6:33/1 Chr 15:13

Father, I declare that You are Lord over my dance. I present my vessel and vehicle to You to live in and move through in any way You please. In my dance, I set You as top and first priority. I set myself to dedicate more time to hearing from You than attending to what song or choreography I will do, what I will wear, or how I will run the ministry. In fact, Lord, You said, if I seek You first, You will add these things to me. If I acknowledge You in my work, You will direct me in what to do. You said if I would commit my works unto You, You would cause my thoughts to become agreeable to Your will. So Lord, I set myself to hear from You. I refuse to commit David's mistake of presumption, when he did not consult You about how You wanted Your matters to be handled. As I seek You, I boldly declare that You are directing my path in dance. I am not confused about what I am to do with the dance or how I am to do it. Your light shines on my path and a voice inside me tells me this is the way, walk in it. I declare my thoughts are agreeable to Your will. I know the pattern You have made for my life in dance and my ministry is built according to that pattern. The songs and the movements I minister are a word in season, because I declare only that which I have heard in my ear from my Lord.

Prov. 16:3 (AMP)

Father, I commit my dancing to You. I declare that you are causing my thoughts to be agreeable to Your will and I have Your thoughts about me/us/dance ministry.

I Ptr. 4:11
When I dance, I dance as God speaking through me. I dance with the ability which God supplies, and in every move of my body God is glorified.

1 Cor. 2:4
I declare the word of God through my dance in demonstration of the Spirit and of His power. The faith of those who are watching me is not in me and my ability, but in the power of God.

1 Cor. 12:27 / 2 Cor. 3:16-17
I am the body of Christ. The Spirit of God uses my dance to declare His works in the earth. He is Lord of my body and when He dances through me, my flesh is taken away and all the people see is Christ.

Acts 13:36
I will fully serve God's will, counsel, and purpose through my dance in my generation.

Jer 1:7-8
I will go to all to whom You send me and I will speak through my dance whatever You command me. I will not fear their faces for I know that You are with me to deliver me.

Jn 14:26
But the Helper, the Holy Spirit, He is teaching me all things about my ministry and my assignment through dance, and He brings to my remembrance all things that He has said to me

Philpns 2:13
God works in me and my dance both to will and to do for *His* good pleasure.

2 Thess 1:12
The name of our Lord Jesus Christ is glorified in me and my dance, and we in Him, according to the grace of our God and the Lord Jesus Christ.

1 Cor. 6:20
I honor God *and* bring glory to Him in my dance.

Ps. 29:1-2
Through my dance, I give unto the LORD glory and strength. I give Him the glory due to His name and I worship Him in the beauty of holiness.

Jn 12:49 / Jn 10:4-5 / Hab 2:1

I declare that when I speak through dance, I do it as one who utters the oracles of God. I set myself to hear what You will say to me. I declare through dance only what I hear in my ear- saying through song and my movements what You have told me to say in the manner You have given me to say it. I do not dance in my own authority. I lay down my wisdom, my ambition, my technique, my experience, my presumptions, my preferences, and my gifting. I lay these all at Your feet and I receive Your strength, which You furnish abundantly. As I declare Your word in Your strength, You are glorified in my dance.

Ministry Leader

John 10:4-5
I know the voice of My Father when He speaks to me regarding this dance ministry and a strangers voice I do not follow. I have a hearing ear and a seeing eye.

Dan. 6:3
[Our dance ministry] distinguishes itself because an excellent spirit is in us.

Neh. 4:6
All who are part of this [dance ministry] have a mind to work.

1 Chr. 28:21
...every willing craftsman is with me for all manner of workmanship, for every kind of service. Those who serve under my stewardship [respect and adhere to the instructions I receive from the Holy Spirit].

2 Chr. 1:10
I have wisdom and knowledge to properly [govern, lead, and administrate] those who are in this ministry under my stewardship.

I Kings 3:9
I have an understanding mind and I am able to govern this ministry excellently and know the difference between right and wrong.

I Cor 1:10 (AMP)
In the name of our Lord Jesus Christ, our dance ministry operates in perfect harmony *and* full agreement in what we say, and there are no dissensions *or* factions *or* divisions among us. We are in full agreement with the leadership of this house and with each other. We are perfectly united in our common understanding, opinions, *and* judgments about the dance ministry and the house-at-large.

Isa. 50:4
We have the spirit of a disciple and one who is taught. Our dances are words in season to this house and wherever we minister.

Acts 4:29
We speak Your word through dance with all boldness and You stretch out Your hand to heal and signs and wonders are done through the name of Jesus.

Mk. 16:20
As we declare the word through dance, the Lord works with us, confirming the word through accompanying signs.

2 Cor. 2:14-15
Through our dance, we diffuse the knowledge of God to the saved and the perishing.

Jn. 15:5
Our ministry remains in God and bears much fruit.

Jn 4:24
We worship God with our dance in spirit and in truth.

Num. 11:17
We declare that we have the same spirit as the leader of this house, and the same spirit of our dance ministry leader.

Isa 30:21
Regarding ministry through my dance, I hear a voice within me saying this is the way, walk in it.

2 Chr 24:13
I am diligent in my dance ministry assignment and things are progressing and growing under me.

Mt. 18:20
Our ministry is gathered together in His name and He is in the midst of us.

Ps. 32:8
Lord You instruct us and teach us in the way our ministry should go. You direct us with Your eye.